636.7
Ne   Nelson, Michael
       The dog repair handbook.

DATE DUE

MR 1 8 '86	AG 3 1 '90	
AP 9 '86	OC 31'90	
JY 10 '86	JY 9'91	
OC 2 '86	NO 2 2 '9	
DE 8 '86	FEB 5 '94	
JA 29 8	APR 27 '94	
MR 2 '87	DEC 1 6	
JY 2 2 87		
JE 18 '88	OCT	
NO 22 '88		
MR 29 '89		
AP 14 '90		

The Dog Repair Handbook

Michael Nelson

The Dog Repair Handbook

The practical guide to canine health care

Macdonald

A Macdonald BOOK

© Michael Nelson 1985
© cartoons Gray Jolliffe 1985

First published in Great Britain in 1985
by Macdonald & Co (Publishers) Ltd
London & Sydney

A member of BPCC plc

British Library Cataloguing in Publication Data

Nelson, Michael, *1929–*
    The dog repair handbook.
    1. Dogs
    I. Title
    636.7'083   SF427

    ISBN 0-356-10833-3

Phototypeset by Acorn Bookwork
Salisbury, Wilts.

Printed and bound in Spain by
Printer Industria Gráfica S.A., Barcelona
D.L.B. 30640-1985

Macdonald & Co (Publishers) Ltd
Maxwell House
74 Worship Street
London EC2A 2EN

Contents

Introduction

Some people are inclined to think that getting a dog is very much like getting a car: select the desired model, fill it with fuel, have an occasional service and that's that.

It might well be in the interests of canine welfare if that were all there were to it, but a dog's life would not be worth living. The truth is that the prospective owner is taking on an obligation that should transcend the simple pride of material possession and which will be around for many years to come.

In any case, dogs do not date in the same way as motor cars. Last year's model looks much the same as this year's and your neighbours' attitude to your pet will depend less on envy than on whether they are dog lovers or not. More importantly, it will also depend on how good an owner you are and whether your training has resulted in a well-balanced, well-behaved dog or a noisy, destructive, canine deliquent.

It is often said that there is no such thing as a bad dog, only a bad owner. As with all generalizations, there are exceptions to the rule, but bad owners certainly exist. This book is written in the fond hope that it will enable the reader to realize his or her full potential and enjoy the benefits of dog ownership and companionship, without the heartbreak that occasionally follows ignorance.

Not that heartbreak is the only trauma you may experience. Ownership can also hit the pocket (perhaps it is rather like owning a car after all). Be consoled by the thought that when you spend money on your dog it is more than repaid by

devotion and the sure knowledge that some member of the human race (perhaps your vet) has moved one step back from the breadline.

There are those who will sometimes wish that they had never embarked on having a dog in much the same way that an exasperated parent in a moment of weakness wishes that a wayward child had never been born. Of course, junior may have been born as a result of a moment of weakness, but let us hope that your pet will have been acquired as a result of less impulsive actions.

Many vets will confirm that an unruly dog is a sure sign that its owner's children are equally uncontrollable. If you are planning to acquire a puppy and cannot yet master your own children, think again. Even more, if your dog is unruly, perhaps you should visit the family planning clinic! In the course of the next hundred pages or so there will be plenty that you need to know about responsible dogmanship. There may even be some things that you do not want to know, but if you have decided that you simply have to have a dog then this book has been written especially for you.

1. Preparing for pooch

It is assumed that you are an intelligent reader and have read the Introduction. If that assumption was wrong, it is now assumed that the error has been amended and the original assumption justified. You will thus appreciate that impulse buying is *infra dig* (if not *infra dog*).

This chapter is therefore written in the fond hope that you have not yet found, acquired or inherited a dog. That may well be a vain hope and you have found this book too late. In that case it is your hard luck and my efforts have been wasted. However, do not skip this chapter as some vital facts will emerge about improving life with your canine friend. In any case, while I am writing for those who are waiting expectantly for these pearls of wisdom *before* taking the plunge, you can eavesdrop and mutter under your breath in agreement from time to time.

First thoughts

Selecting a dog takes time and trouble. That appealing bundle of fluff in the shop window can undergo metamorphosis into a smelly, hair-shedding horror story that you would never have dreamed of taking on board had you spared the time to think about it.

It (we have not yet considered the sex of the specimen you plan to acquire) is going to be a member of your family for its lifetime, and it is the one member of the family that you can actually choose. You may think that you chose your spouse, but fate (some might say doom) undoubtedly played a large part in that. Your children arrive as a result of a fantastic lottery in which the permutations of genes involved are infinitely more complicated than the treble chance in the football pools – but with rather more chance of hitting the jackpot, and with fewer entries, at that.

The opportunity of making the correct

choice must be grasped firmly, taking various factors into account. Sex (or rather gender, perhaps), size, type of coat, purchase price, maintenance costs (including repairs, modifications and fuel consumption), basic or de luxe model and the purpose for which the dog is intended (pet, breeding, working or show, or even all four) are all factors to be carefully considered.

However, there is one other factor that is even more important – your suitability as an owner. Is it at all possible that you might not be prepared to devote the time and attention necessarily demanded of a responsible owner? Responsible dogmanship demands that you commit yourself to the interests of your dog. In return, you may expect your efforts to be repaid many times over. The following pages are designed to assist you in finding out whether you deserve to have a dog, and if so to choose the right one.

Responsible dogmanship

Although there are some similarities between rearing children and puppies, there are also differences. It is infinitely easier to contemplate a family when you know that there will come a time when they are able to keep themselves clean, brush their own hair and even be helpful about the house if you are very lucky.

On the other hand, you do not have to change nappies for a puppy. It is just liable to make messes in the most awkward places about the house, such as on a new carpet or just where you put your bare foot when you get out of bed in the morning (that, by the way, is one very good reason for not letting a puppy sleep in your bedroom).

From the moment you arrive home with a new puppy under your arm, you are committing yourself to its training, feeding and exercise, all of which take a considerable amount of time. You are also committing yourself to keeping it company. It is not considered right to leave children on their own – in fact it can be disastrous – and it is equally wrong to treat a dog in the same way. A dog, especially a puppy, needs attention.

Dogs are pack animals and they need to become aware of their position in the pecking order in the social group in which they find themselves. If it is allowed to have its own way you will find your dog becoming master of you, and not vice versa. On the other hand, if you and your family establish the right relationship with your pet, you can count on loyalty, companionship, a personal security service and, in addition, somebody to take you out for walks.

Dogmanship cannot be regarded as a one-sided business. Your dog has every reason to expect advantages from owning a human being. It is canine nature to want one of those lanky, two-legged creatures that can be such fun, even if they have to be humoured at play, like running after a ball when it is thrown and bringing it back to their feet, time and time again. Your dog will be consoled by the knowledge that mere humans usually get tired of playing first.

Both sides of the partnership have to work hard some of the time, but it is your

dog that usually has the time to spare. That, of course, is just as it should be since the partnership's financial backing comes from the human element who, one hopes, has it to spare – which balances the equation nicely.

The DAT

Before you can drive a car without supervision you must gain a full licence by passing a driving test. In many countries it is necessary to have a licence if you own a dog, although you do not have to pass a test before you are allowed out alone in charge of your four-legged companion. However, as a contribution to canine knowledge there follows a simple test – the DAT, Dogmanship Aptitude Test – designed to see whether you make the grade in the dogmanship stakes.

What is your DATing rating?

Answer the questions with absolute honesty and record a, b or c for each one, 1 to 10. Refer to page 12 for the scores and add up your marks. Here goes, then:

1. If your neighbours' dog barks every time they go out and leave it at home, do you
a) complain to the police
b) offer to look after it
c) ask them to take it out with them?

2. If your spouse suggests that you both go out for a walk do you
a) leap at the chance
b) turn a deaf ear and change the subject
c) say you are expecting a phone call?

3. Is there someone at home
a) most of the day and night
b) at least half the day
c) not during working hours?

4. Does your home look
a) lived in
b) immaculate
c) a rubbish tip?

5. How much time could you devote to your dog on an average day
a) none
b) one hour
c) half an hour?

6. Is your temperament
a) calm and equable
b) volatile
c) reasonable most of the time?

7. Is your bank manager
a) pleased to have you as a customer
b) always writing you threatening letters
c) only mildly co-operative?

8. Have you checked on vet fees in your area?
a) no
b) yes
c) you are so rich that it does not matter

9. Do you have
a) a large enough garden for your dog
b) a park near by where you can exercise it
c) a house in the country?

10. Do you frequently
a) oversleep
b) get up earlier than you need to
c) get your spouse up early to do the chores?

The maximum possible score is 100, but on the other hand if you are the eldest son of an earl or some other pedigree stock, living in the family mansion, you could legitimately score 30 on Question 9 as places like Woburn Abbey are houses in the country with large gardens and not only near, but IN, a large park. In that case the maximum score would be 120. And if your answer to Question 8, on veterinary fees, was that you are so rich they do not bother you, why are you not one of *my* clients?

A rating of 80 or more suggests that you are likely to exhibit responsible dogmanship to a high degree. Fifty to 75 rates you as about an acceptable owner who, if you work at it (and, of course, read through this book to the end), could enhance your rating in due course. Those who scored less than 50 have failed, at least this time around, and should consider a less demanding occupation such as cake decorating or breeding hamsters. But whatever the score, you should now analyse the results of your rating.

1. Why is it that the only people with perfect neighbours happen to live next door to us? If you are ready to be considerate to neighbours who offend you there is a fair chance that you will do your best to ensure you do not offend them. The first lesson is to realize that dutiful dogmanship entails earning the goodwill of the non-dog-owning public.

2. Assuming a nil score on this one, it may be that you simply do not like your spouse enough to go for a walk, but if it is because you are lazy then do not delude yourself that a dog will galvanize you into activity. You can either trade this book in for a collection of crossword puzzles or buy yourself a goldfish.

3. It goes without saying that a dog should not be left alone all day. Furthermore, a puppy needs a lot of time expended on its house-training and in establishing from the beginning the difference between right and wrong.

Dating rating scores

QUESTION	1	2	3	4	5	6	7	8	9	10
score 10	b	a	a	a	b	a	a	a/c	all	b
score 5	c	–	b	c	c	c	c	–	–	c
score 0	a	b	c	b	a	b	b	b	–	a

4. It does not follow that keeping a dog means that your home will be ruined or become a malodorous dump, but if you are so house-proud that everything has to be perfect, forget about having a dog. Conversely, a rubbish tip presents hazards for all concerned.

5. The amount of time that it takes to look after a dog properly can vary with size and breed. The time may even exceed one hour per day depending on ease of grooming and the amount of exercise needed.

6. With luck you will not need to be patient all the time, but you will achieve more by being kind and firm than by being irascible.

7. You cannot get away from the fact that keeping dogs costs money. Food is a regular, day-in day-out expense unless your pet stops eating. In that case you will have a vet's bill instead.

8. Veterinary fees are not as high as most people think. If you think they are more than you can afford, ask the vet about insurance to cover fees.

9. As pointed out earlier, there is a need for exercise.

10. Somebody should get up in the morning to let the dog out!

Dog selection

Now that you are about to give yourself the seal of approval as a dog owner, you should consider next what type of dog to get. A common failing is to try to pick out a breed first (although, if you insist, turn to page 131 for some suggestions). Unless you are sure of the breed you want, it is better to consider other aspects beforehand.

What size?

This is really the first step in the process of elimination. Size of dog may be dictated to some extent by the size of your residence, and if you live in a small house or in a flat then you should rule out the larger breeds.

However, there are other considerations and you do not have to choose a large breed simply because you live in a large house. For example, someone of small stature would probably be unwise to buy a Great Dane and equally an owner over 6 feet tall might look rather ridiculous with, say, a Chihuahua. Another point to remember is that picking a large

breed when you have only a small garden is going to increase the amount of walking you have to undertake in the neighbourhood, and that is over and above the extra exercise that large breeds need compared to the smaller ones. So unless exercise is your forte, go for the smaller dogs.

Do not forget that from time to time you will have to take the dog in your car. It might even be so ill that you have to carry it out to the car and lay it in the back, flat out. If yours is a two-door car, either get a small dog or start saving for a truss or orthopaedic bed right now.

Long- or short-coated?

Grooming short-coated dogs is less time-consuming than attending to those with longer coats. Likewise, they need bathing less often and, as a bonus, tend to bring less dirt into the house. Having bathed the dog, it is much easier to dry one with a short coat. In fact, it is rather like the difference between a drip-dry and an ironed cotton shirt: the one is much easier to deal with but the other is so much more attractive until it is soiled.

Pedigree, crossbred or mongrel?

Now that you have decided on size and type of coat, and assuming no colour prejudice, you can narrow down the search to a selection of breeds or breed types.

The problem with mongrels, and often with crossbreds as well, is that their pups may well tend to grow into something bearing no similarity to the mother, let alone the father (always supposing that he is known). A pedigree dog, on the other hand, will cost more than a mongrel and show breed quality more than pet quality. Some breeds command higher prices, based on scarcity value which can also be influenced by popularity, and a few have hereditary problems that can be troublesome to the dog and expensive for the owner.

Before you make a final decision on a breed, consult your vet (if you have one by now) or a knowledgeable owner, and read some breed manuals. Then prepare for an on-site inspection.

Dog or bitch?

The first question to ask yourself here is whether you want a litter of puppies in due course. If the answer is 'yes', then there is not much point in buying a male, but bear in mind that breeding is not something to be entered into lightly. Having a bitch that comes into heat for three weeks every six months, acting as a magnet for all the neighbourhood canine Casanovas, may not be everyone's idea of heaven. Before making a final decision you should check through Chapter 8, where sex and breeding are explained in some detail.

Not all male dogs are very aware of the phallic function, possibly because they spend so much time cocking their legs that they forget about it. Others are only too well aware of it but can become tiresomely confused about the proper object of their attentions. However, most dogs can lead a celibate existence quite happily and without attempting to rush off looking for a bitch as soon as your back is turned.

There is a tendency for bitches to be rather more gentle than males, but this is not a hard and fast rule. If you are planning to acquire your very first dog, then it comes down to a matter of personal preference rather than dogmatism. On the other hand, if you already have one dog and it has not been neutered, then you would be better picking another of the same sex.

Source of supply

Ask any vet where you should go to buy a puppy and the answer will always be from a breeder. This is because it is assumed that you want a dog as free of disease as possible. Buying direct means that the only stress the puppy will face is that of the transfer from its mother and littermates to your home. If you buy from a pet store or puppy farm it will already have had one such stress and possibly will still be in shock when you arrive on the scene.

It may be that you would prefer to have an adult rather than a puppy, perhaps because you would like to give a good home to a deprived dog that might otherwise be put down. It is as well to be sure it *is* indeed deprived and not depraved: is it destructive in the home, vicious or inadequately trained? You should not take on anything of the kind, even for free. A second-hand dog is rarely worth any money, and most owners would be more concerned about whether it was going to a good home rather than filthy lucre. There are a number of organizations that try to place such dogs. In Britain there are the Royal Society for the Prevention of Cruelty to Animals and local homes for stray dogs, and practically every breed society runs a breed rescue service.

Quite apart from making a contribution to animal welfare in offering a home to an unwanted adult, there are some other reasons for considering a mature specimen. Senior citizens may not be able to cope with an exuberant pup, especially when it is older, unless it is a small breed. In general terms, however, it is probably better to take on a puppy, if only to start it out in the way you mean to go on.

What to look for when buying

Having decided after due consideration exactly what kind of puppy you want to acquire and established the source, you are off to pick out your own addition to the family, armed with cheque-book or a handful of banknotes.

The object is to find a puppy that will grow into a healthy, happy, well-behaved but outgoing dog or bitch. It may not be all that easy to tell when a pup is only a few weeks old, but one of the best guides is to meet the parents. If you are going to a breeder (another good reason for buying direct from the manufacturer) you will, at least, have the opportunity of meeting Mum. It is even possible that Dad could be on the premises as well, but Mum may originally have been sent away to stud.

Ask to see the Mum (and Dad, if there) *before* meeting the litter. When a bitch meets strangers with her litter there, her behaviour may be out of character. It is easy to tell whether she is friendly or not, whether she is nervous, lacking confidence or the kind of dog you are looking for. Likewise with the sire, if he is around.

Now ask to see the litter. Go in gently and take your time. Let the puppies come up to you. They may be asleep when you first meet them (like all babies, puppies sleep a lot), so allow a little time for them to get their bearings. If they all come up to you as soon as they are aware of you there is little to choose between them as far as temperament is concerned, but beware of the little fellow skulking in the corner. You may take pity on him but shyness is not an endearing quality in the adult dog, and it could be that the retiring pup is none too well.

It is vital to select a fit puppy. You have probably earmarked one by now that has the right temperament, is of the right sex and, if you are looking for perfection, a good specimen of the breed. Check that its eyes and nose are clear of any discharge and have a quick look at the other end to ensure that it is free of the tell-tale signs of diarrhoea. There should be no sign of lameness and the coat should be even, with no bald patches or excessive irritation. The ears should be clean, although a small amount of dark brown wax is of little significance. It may mean ear mites, but this problem can be easily dealt with in due course (see page 100).

If you have chosen a puppy that is not yet old enough to leave its mother, then when you go to collect it in a few weeks do make sure that it is still in the same state of health as when you last saw it.

Preparing for pup's arrival

The day was when the dog had to make do with what it got. After all, the owner did not have all that much for the family. An old coat to lie on in the garden-shed or a makeshift outdoor kennel (and in some cases that was just about all there was for the kids) was the most it could expect.

In those bad old days the dog got the scraps left over from the family's meal and some biscuits to make up the bulk. Nowadays, the affluent society has penetrated the domestic animal kingdom too. There is a complete range of dog beds of all shapes and sizes, coats to keep them warm in centrally heated rooms, a variety of bowls and dishes and such a range of convenience foods, health foods and vegetarian rations that you wonder how we poor humans used to manage.

Not that you shouldn't prepare for the new arrival, of course. The first essentials are to plan where and on what it is going to sleep and where and from what it is going to eat and drink. Then see that everything is ready *before* the pup arrives. A young puppy can create instant havoc, as many an unprepared owner will testify. It has an insatiable desire to chew, rip and shred everything it can lay its razor-sharp little teeth on, except, of course, for the dog chews you bought especially for that purpose.

From the start, you should accept that anything left within reach may and probably will be destroyed. If you are the absent-minded type who has difficulty in remembering to put things away, do not just think of the cost of replacing chewed

shoes and shredded cushions – consider the vet's charges for removing an assortment of unlikely objects from your puppy's insides.

Where to sleep?

Sleeping facilities do not pose much of a problem with an adult dog as it will not sleep anything like as much as a puppy during the day. Nevertheless, it is still only fair to provide a haven for those moments of peace and quiet that we all look for at times. If you are getting a pup it is much more important to provide one place where it can rest, day and night, without being disturbed by rush-hour traffic as its human companions bustle their way about the house.

Ideally, indeed, dogs are better kept outside the house in draught-free sheds or kennels. Even apparently frail lap-dogs do not need the centrally heated luxury to which we have accustomed ourselves. After all, they are born with fur coats and can cope with cold conditions far better than the average owner thinks.

However, not everyone has the facilities outside to provide the ideal conditions and some people may even have difficulty in finding a place indoors. Besides, many owners are unable to accept the idea of sending a new member of the family to take up residence in the coal-shed. Inside, there is a great temptation to put the pup's bed next to the kitchen boiler. This should be avoided if at all possible. Quite apart from the heat being unnecessary, undesirable and positively harmful, boilers can be noisy. Solid fuel boilers have to be stoked, and gas- or oil-fired ones tend to have minor explosions when they come on. The result can be disturbance for the dog and sleepless nights for you.

You should choose a place where the dog can escape from interfering people, especially children, more especially toddlers. We all have the desire for our own little territory where we can retreat and escape from the trials and tribulations of the world. Your dog will be no exception.

If you can offer a puppy a den of its own within the kitchen precincts, better still in a scullery (it is usually cooler), away from human traffic lanes, you will be giving it a good start. All you have to do is convince the pup that it should feel the same way about its prospective quarters as you do. One way to encourage this is to have some means of enclosure, such as a play-pen, but remember to leave enough room to permit access to the area set aside for toilet-training. A puppy is (fortunately) usually reluctant to perform its natural functions in its own sleeping quarters and good hygiene is to be encouraged. With luck this habit will be gradually extended to your entire house, provided you are patient.

What kind of bed?

If you are buying a small breed it is a simple matter to buy a suitable bed in time for the pup's arrival. Larger breeds, on the other hand, will swiftly outgrow any puppy-sized bed and, unless you are scandalously rich, you should prepare some DIY accommodation for the first few months.

Puppies tend to be a little unpredictable in their tastes, but there is much to be said for making use of those cartons you get from your friendly neighbourhood supermarket. They have the advantage of being disposable and not just cheap but free. Either cut down the side, leaving a 'step' at the bottom to retain the bedding, or cut a circular hole in the side at puppy height, rather like a nesting box but with a hole big enough for a puppy rather than a bird.

Feeding and watering

We shall be dealing with feeding in more detail in the next chapter, but it is the custom for a breeder or pet-store owner to provide a diet sheet with every puppy sold. This is a perfectly sensible idea, although some diet sheets say more about the pretensions of the breeder – so be prepared to be cynical. A useful sheet will, at least, tell you what the diet has

been based on hitherto, but then it is highly likely that you will change to something less time consuming but just as nutritious in due course, probably of the packaged variety.

Whatever the prospective menu, you will need something to serve it in. Food dishes and water bowls are essential. In the first place they should be kept quite separate from the dishes used by the rest of the household (although hospitalization is unlikely to occur should an accident happen) and secondly it is strongly recommended that the dog's dishes have a heavy base so they cannot be tipped over easily nor pushed around the floor. Water must be available at all times, but preferably within the bowl! Therefore avoid bowls with sloping sides. Perpendicular sides with a small overlap help to avoid spillage when lapping. An overhanging rim is less suitable for feeding bowls, making it harder for the dog to get at the food without snuffling about, but a certain amount of depth is necessary to stop the food being pushed on to the floor.

Grooming needs

Do not rush out and buy grooming aids until you know what type of dog you are going to get, and even then a puppy's coat is not necessarily going to be the same as that of an adult. Admittedly grooming is a chore, but one you should begin soon after acquisition so that a puppy gets used to the procedure while it is still of manageable size and temper.

This is particularly important in a long-coated breed, which needs more

time spent on titivation than those with short coats. There are many proud owners of puppies who end up as disenchanted owners of dogs because they could not spare the time to brush and comb their charge, which consequently developed a snaggled, matted covering of knots and tangles – and a rigorous aversion to having them brushed out. Unfortunately, some of the breeds most prone to this problem have become extremely popular. The Old English Sheepdog is a prime example. Freshly laundered it looks absolutely superb; inadequately cared for it looks more like an old English sheep – and smells rather worse.

The person from whom you are buying your puppy will be the best one to advise you on what grooming aids are suitable for your chosen breed, unless it is short-coated, in which case a simple brush and comb will be all that you need to start with.

Finding the vet

The last thing to do is to wait until you need a vet before looking for one. A veterinary surgeon will be an *essential* part of the life of your pet at some time or another, and you may well need one in some dire emergency. The emergency will be less dire, or at least easier to cope with, if you already know whom to call for help.

Of course, you can always turn to a local listings, put on a blindfold and stick a pin in the page. If that is the way you found your family doctor and you were satisfied with the result, go ahead. You are either easily satisfied or were very lucky. If it was the latter, your luck is just about to run out!

It is difficult to know what it is that gives confidence in the practitioner of some profession or craft, but one or more of a number of factors may be involved. Charm, panache, an ability to listen to your problems and understand your needs, the ability to put you and your pet at ease and, of course, success are just some of the qualitites to look for in a vet. The premises are not necessarily all that important, but there must be some minimum standard that is acceptable to you – a clean waiting-room and helpful staff, for a start.

If you do not know any veterinarians in your area already, ask all your pet-owning friends whom they go to and what they think of the service. This will enable you to hear more than one opinion, if only to show that what pleases one person does not always please another. However, remember that your friends' judgement may be influenced by the fees charged!

Now, totally confused, you can either decide to discard their opinions and strike out on your own or weigh up all the evidence and make your choice. A preliminary visit to spy out the land may well be worthwhile, perhaps on the pretext of enquiring about the cost of puppy vaccinations.

Most practices include a health check for the puppy at its first visit to the surgery in their vaccination fees. If you are going to compare fees, establish which diseases are being covered and the number of visits to the surgery required so that you can compare like with like. At the same time you can find out the surgery hours and whether there is an appointment system. If the vet runs open surgeries (in which appointments are not needed) you may well find that he or she prefers to see young animals by appointment outside surgery hours until they have completed their vaccination course, in order to avoid the risk of contact with sick pets. No puppy should be brought into contact with other dogs until its vaccinations are complete and its immunity to infectious diseases fully established.

are setting off to collect your new puppy. Don't panic! Instead, prepare yourself calmly for the safe collection of your pet. This is really no problem if you are going by car, but if travelling by public transport it is as well to have a sturdily made pet carrier. Obviously this must be large enough to put the puppy in, but not so large that it cannot be conveniently placed on your knees during the journey. It should also have an impervious base in order to protect your knees – and perhaps other passengers – should your new acquisition prove incontinent during transit.

Remember that if the weather is inclement the carrier should protect the pup from wind and rain. After all, if you do not want the pup to wet you, why should the puppy not want to keep dry too, even if it is only rain!

Collecting your puppy

The great day has arrived and now you

Check your pup

If you are returning to collect a pup that you originally chose when it was too young to leave its mother, go through the inspection procedure a second time. A dull and dejected pup or one showing discharge of the eyes or nose, or any indication of diarrhoea, should be rejected. This applies even if you have selected it earlier and paid a deposit. You contracted to purchase a healthy puppy, and no matter how disappointed you or your family may be, no matter how sorry you feel for the puppy, it is not in its best interests to remove it from its mother and littermates until it is in perfect health and able to withstand the stress of moving to a new home.

What to ask your supplier

There are a number of vital pieces of information that you ought to know before you leave for home with the pup. To begin with, the breeder should tell you its date of birth, and if the information is not forthcoming then ask for it – the vet will need to know the date of birth when he comes to give the pup its first vaccination. Pedigree dogs may have been registered with the Kennel Club (or other appropriate body if purchased outside the British Isles), in which case you should be give a registration certificate and a pedigree. Sometimes the breeder may not have completed the pedigree document and will promise to send it on. Make sure that he does, for you will need the document should you ever wish to breed from the dog.

Check whether the puppy has already had its first dose of vaccine. Some breeders have this done before a puppy is sold so that it is less likely to contract an infection during its first few weeks in a new home. The cost will have either been included in the purchase price or added as an extra. In either case you should be supplied with a vaccination certificate signed by a veterinarian. This will specify the diseases covered by the vaccine used. Some breeders have their puppies vaccinated against only canine parvovirus, in which case you should consult your vet about the best age to start vaccination against the rest of the diseases. See Chapter 6 for more details about vaccinations and the infections they guard against.

Do not forget to ask your supplier about the grooming equipment you will need and the details of any worming treatments already given. No doubt you will be advised of the supplier's opinions on worming – with luck not in tiresome detail – but you should still discuss this with the vet on your first visit as not all breeders are sufficiently aware of the need for repeated worming up to six months of age. The most important thing is to know when the last worming dose was given.

Finally, unless the supplier provides you with a feeding chart, ask about the puppy's current diet. The important details are what it is being fed each day, how much and when. In fact you should find this out when you first make arrangements to collect the pup so that you can nip out and stock up beforehand.

Unless you have forgotten your wallet, you are now ready to pick up pup and make the journey home; and if you are travelling by car rather than public transport, the vital importance of an impervious box comes into its own. In a car, a dog is likely to be sick as well as incontinent and the mess is best confined to a sturdy container – and do not make the mistake of keeping an eye only on the pup's rear end!

A pup's new home

You thought the journey home was fun? Just you wait for the first night in your house! To begin with your puppy will find all sorts of interesting smells, a complete new world in which the centre of attraction is itself. There will be food offered without half a dozen other tiny mouths trying to gain possession of the same bowl. There will be a bed to sleep in and a clean floor uncontaminated by the mess of all the littermates. How long it remains clean is another matter!

Come night-time, however, and pooch is going to wish for the warmth and comfort of the family that was left behind at the kennels. If you want an undisturbed night you had better try to help pooch overcome homesickness. Remember that the puppy has not slept alone before, indeed is used to cuddling into the warm bodies of the rest of the litter and of

mother. The puppy will also be used to the steady sound of its mother's heartbeat. The use of a hot-water bottle under a layer of blanket will provide the warmth and a loud ticking alarm clock under several layers can simulate the mother's heartbeat, but do make sure the alarm is not set!

If you really want to secure an undisturbed night ensure that the puppy is tired before settling down by keeping it going without sleep during the day. Give a good feed about half an hour before bedtime, let it use its toilet area and then get ready for a sleep. Put out the light and tiptoe off to bed yourself, fingers crossed.

Learning independence

One of the most important lessons of its new life that a pup should learn is that it cannot expect to be in the company of others all day, every day. Obviously, a growing puppy cannot be left on its own for too long as it needs feeding and house-training, but some owners are tempted to let a pup accompany them all over the house. This is a mistake. Make the puppy accept from the outset that there are times when it is restricted to its own den, even if the owners are about.

Once the puppy is used to this idea, you are but a short step from teaching it to accept that it will be left on its own while you go out of the house. As long as it has regular mealtimes and is given the opportunity to perform its natural functions (usually shortly after meals) in the place that makes *you* happy, a puppy will soon adjust to your house rules.

Exercise and play

An irritating problem in the early days is that while a pup will need to be exercised, you cannot take it for a walk in areas where it is likely to meet other dogs until its vaccinations are complete. In fact, the 'problem' is really more of an excuse to put your feet up, because strenuous exercise should be limited until a pup has grown and developed. Play provides most of the exercise a pup needs and should cease when it shows signs of being tired.

As for going out, providing your garden is used only by your own dogs (and they have been vaccinated), there is no reason why your puppy should not be exercised in it – weather permitting and under supervision. However, you need to be particularly careful that the garden is dog-proof, not only to keep pooch in but also to keep other dogs out. Never underestimate the Houdini-like qualities that pups can demonstrate when you least expect it. If you think that escape becomes less likely as they grow too big for the small gaps, those delusions will disappear when you find that pups also grow stronger as they grow bigger. The small gaps grow into big ones at an even faster rate than the dog grows. This is probably because as the dog grows it actually *wants* to get out and investigate pastures new, whereas with a puppy it is really all a matter of chance. A puppy is much more likely to escape as the result of a lucky blunder through the fence than by an act of deliberate canine delinquency.

Settling in

By now you will appreciate that the process of getting a puppy involves a large measure of adaptation. Your life for a start, the house for another, then the garden but above all for the puppy.

Until you came on the scene the pup's life had been one of eating, making messes, playing and sleeping, eating, making messes, playing and sleeping and so on. The eating, playing and sleeping are very acceptable, but the toilet activity starts to pall after a few days unless you are fortunate enough to have chosen a puppy that is either naturally clean or a quick learner, although how many proud owners would readily admit that theirs was neither?

2. Settling in

A disposable object is intended to be discarded at the end of its short life. Unless you are extraordinarily mean, you would waste neither time nor money on keeping such a thing in good working order.

However, an object with moving parts, such as a car or washing machine, needs a certain amount of care spent on it. Keeping it clean and supplied with energy does not involve any maintenance but constitutes the bare minimum for its function. An occasional but regular check of the main functional systems can avoid time, trouble and money in curing problems that could have been averted if spotted earlier.

It is just the same with your dog. A regular check of mouth, nose, ears, eyes and the exhaust system will give advance warning of trouble ahead. Perhaps you know enough about your car or

washing machine to make minor repairs yourself. The great thing is to know your limitations and when to call in the experts. It is easy to try a little adjustment here and there with an engine, and you can always switch an engine off when your efforts have made things worse. If you switch your dog off, you will not switch it on again!

Accepting those limitations, what *can* you do? This chapter covers general maintenance. General repairs will be dealt with later when you know a little more.

Nutrition

All animals require food and water for maintenance of life-support functions, the wherewithal to grow and/or replace body tissues and to provide the energy for day-to-day activities. Some animals have specific needs for their diet. The cat, for example, is unable to utilize vegetable protein effectively, which explains why canned cat foods are more expensive than canned dog foods.

The Fates have therefore smiled on the dog owner and provided the dog with a digestive system that can utilize the cheaper vegetable proteins and thus cut down the food bill. Alternatively, the

Fates have smiled upon the pet food industry and compensated it for the lower food consumption of cats, compared to the dog, by ensuring that cats run only on the most expensive five-star fuel!

Your dog can virtually eat anything (and probably will if you are not careful) and derive *some* nutritional benefit as long as it is capable of being digested and is non-toxic. This is not to say that you *should* feed *anything* to your dog. It still needs a balanced diet and you need to know what to give it, unless you are already a canine dietician. The following pages are intended to help you understand your dog's needs, and after that there follows advice on how best to meet them.

Dietary needs

Dogs need protein, fat, carbohydrate, water, vitamins and minerals at levels that replace those excreted from the body or used in maintaining body functions, including growth and repair.

Protein
This is the major constituent of body cells and constitutes about 20 per cent of the dog's weight. It is recommended that a diet contain 20 per cent of the dry matter as protein. The growing pup, the elderly dog and the pregnant bitch have greater protein requirements than the younger or middle-aged adult. This need is generally met by increased food intake rather than modifying the diet.

Fat
Fat requirements are adequately met by provision of 10 per cent mixed vegetable and animal fats. Apart from being a valuable source of energy, fats contain a number of essential substances called fatty acids. These can either be 'saturated' fatty acids (derived from animal fats) or 'unsaturated' fatty acids (derived from vegetable fats). Why they are so called is unimportant, the point is that they are essential in maintaining health. There is usually no deficiency of saturated fatty acids in the diet of most dogs, but a dry, harsh, staring coat with scaly skin, not unlike dandruff, may well indicate a deficiency of unsaturated fatty acids.

Carbohydrates
Carbohydrates or starchy foods provide

energy. Protein can also be used as a source of energy, but is not as readily broken down in the body as fat and carbohydrate for that purpose. If, for example, the level of exercise is increased, the additional energy intake is best met by extra carbohydrate or fat in the diet rather than protein. Conversely, if exercise is reduced, lower the fat or carbohydrate intake. On the other hand, if a dog has been overfed on a balanced diet and needs slimming it is as well to reduce the whole diet, protein and all.

As carbohydrates are vegetable in origin, carbohydrate-rich foods tend to be cheaper than the high-protein (meat-based) products.

Water
This makes up the greatest part of the dog's body, being over 60 per cent of its weight. It should not be forgotten that owners are also over 60 per cent water. Water output must be balanced by water intake if you are to maintain good health. Excessive fluid intake will be followed inevitably by an equally increased output, usually as urine. Remember when preparing a meal for your dog that meat is around 60 per cent water before it is cooked; roasting will reduce water content but a stew has an increased water content. Requirements for water increase in hot weather and reduce in cold. The provision of ample water is essential and a fresh supply should always be available for a healthy dog.

It is not difficult to keep a check on water intake, as after keeping the water bowl filled for a month or two you will have a good idea of young hound's daily needs. Any sudden increase may indicate that something is wrong, and unless it is wet underfoot or there are signs of diarrhoea, have a look outside. You never know, there may be a heatwave on its way!

Roughage
Roughage or dietary fibre is desirable in the food of simple-stomached animals such as the dog (and, indeed, man too) to provide texture and bulk to faeces. Roughage consists of cellulose – the walls of plant cells – and it passes down the gut undigested. Two per cent roughage in the diet will be sufficient to prevent the soft, stinking motion that follows a diet of meat alone.

Vitamins
These are essential for health in dog and man alike. If any vitamins are lacking in the diet and the animal cannot synthesize them, signs of a deficiency will soon appear. The effects vary, depending on the identity of the missing vitamin and its function in the body. Vitamin A, for example, is involved in bone formation, the maintenance of skin and mucous membranes and their ability to resist infection, as well as being necessary for normal vision. The vitamin B complex is involved in a whole range of body functions, especially digestive and respiratory activity. Vitamin B12 is essential for the formation of red blood cells and a deficiency leads to pernicious anaemia.

Vitamin C is synthesized naturally by the dog and is unnecessary in its diet. Humans, on the other hand, need their orange juice. Vitamin D is involved with vitamin A in bone growth. Both vitamins A and D are derived from animal sources, so if a dog is fed on a vegetarian diet it is vital to supplement these two vitamins. Some vitamin A requirements can be met by eating plants containing the pigment beta-carotene as the dog can convert it to Vitamin A, but this may not be sufficient for its needs. Liver is rich in both vitamins A and D. Vitamin E is essential for certain processes in the body concerned with muscles and with reproduction.

Minerals

Minerals are equally as important as food and vitamins. There are some 20 essential minerals, a number of which need only to be present in minute amounts. As far as these 'trace' elements are concerned, most needs are satisfied by any mixed animal and plant diet.

The only minerals that need concern us are calcium, iodine, iron, potassium, phosphorus and sodium. Even then, virtually all diets with meat and vegetables will provide adequate levels of iodine, iron, potassium and sodium. That leaves calcium and phosphorus which are important for bone formation of the growing puppy and during pregnancy and lactation in the bitch.

The ratio of calcium to phosphorus in the diet should be balanced within certain limits. As they occur naturally in bone in the right kind of proportions, the intelligent thing to do would be to add bone to the diet. However, before you dash out to the potting-shed to raid your horticultural supplies, it must be pointed out that for your dog's health it is advisable to feed *sterile* bone flour. Include it as 3 per cent of the daily ration (as dry matter) if you are preparing your own foods for your pet. If you are buying pet foods made by a reputable manufacturer you are unlikely to need much in the way of vitamin and mineral supplements as the food should already contain the right amounts.

However, it could well be that your chosen diet is not as complete as you think. Some dog foods do not have any declared levels of vitamin and mineral content and supplementation is obviously required, even though label declarations may claim that the diet is complete when fed according to directions. If in doubt then ask the supplier, manufacturer or your vet. The reliable manufacturer keeps your vet informed about its products and can advise you on any supplement that may be necessary.

Some foods may have guaranteed vitamin levels for a limited period of time and will have an expiry date on them. Bear this in mind if purchasing your dog food in bulk.

Vitamin and mineral supplements

There is a plethora of tablets and powders on the market under a variety of brand names and it is by no means easy to choose the most suitable one for your dog. Quite apart from the variation in pack sizes, concentration of the various constituents will vary from product to product, together with the dose rate. When selecting your supplements,

compare these points to ensure that you get value for money and take particular ·care to use the contents before the expiry date on the label has been reached.

Types of dog food

Although we have known for a long time how much protein, fat and carbohydrate a dog needs in its diet, much of our detailed knowledge of canine nutrition is due to the efforts of the major pet food companies to produce the ideal dog food. Using modern scientific techniques, we now know that some substances which were previously thought to be poisonous are essential for health, albeit in very small amounts.

The reputable pet food manufacturers endeavour to ensure that their products will satisfy all essential needs. It is possible to feed a dog a balanced ration using any number of different raw materials, but there is much to be said for the prepared convenience foods.

There is also no doubt that ailments due to dietary deficiency are less common nowadays because more dogs are fed on prepared foods than on the often ill-balanced rations of home-prepared fresh foods or household scraps.

These convenience foods are of three basic types: the dry expanded diet with 10 per cent water content; the semi-moist packaged foods with 15–25 per cent water; and canned foods with 75–80 per cent water.

Canned foods

Do not be too shocked by the high water content in canned foods. Fresh meat has a 60 per cent water content and it is bound to be increased with gravy and jelly.

The canned foods are generally of two types: those with cereals already mixed in to make a kind of luncheon-meat texture designed to be a complete food and, secondly, a meat-and-gravy type intended to be fed with biscuit or a biscuit meal. It is usual to include a certain amount of textured soya in the 'meat', but this is good digestible protein.

The meaty canned foods are very palatable and those with added cereal are usually well accepted by even the most selective dog. Shelf-life is at least a year until the can is opened, when it is safe to feed over the next 24 hours provided the can is stored in a fridge. To be on the safe side, remove the meat from the can before putting it in the fridge, using a special container for the purpose clearly labelled 'DOG FOOD' to avoid famished members of the family raiding it for sandwiches between meals! In the event that they cannot read use a picture of a dog instead.

Semi-moist foods

These complete diets are easily stored in their original packages in the larder and have a shelf-life of about six months. They are highly palatable to dogs and to young children, so keep them on the top shelf out of reach of both!

Dry expanded diets

The complete dry foods consist of meat meal, soya, fish meal, cereals and fat with a six-month shelf-life. Not all dogs find them attractive as their sole diet, but the mixtures will satisfy their nutritional needs. These foods should not be confused with the expanded mixer meals made from cereals and fat which are designed to be mixed with protein diets, such as meat, in the same way as biscuits and biscuit meals.

Other foods

Before leaving the subject of prepared foods mention must be made of some of the others you can see in pet stores. For example, there are some specially manufactured brawns and sausage-like foods which are usually preserved with sodium sulphite and have a limited shelf-life. With a maximum life of two weeks once opened and an unknown time on display in the pet store it is wisest to buy either an unopened pack or one day's requirements at a time.

There are also some protein concentrate and cereal mixes that prove very acceptable to some dogs and are claimed to satisfy dietary requirements. Watch expiry dates on the packaging as vitamin levels are guaranteed only up to that time.

How much to feed?

It is impossible to state just how much a dog should eat for its weight as there can be considerable variation between individuals, even from the same litter. We all know of people who eat everything they want and never put on weight whereas most of us put it on at the drop of a hat.

As long as we are not greedy, we tend to eat just what we need and instinctively adjust our food intake accordingly. So it is with dogs. The only problem is that if our needs increase we can help ourselves to some more, whereas the dog depends on what it is given. Apart from the basic metabolic rate – the measure of energy needed to maintain an individual with neither gain nor loss in weight – energy needs will also vary with the amount of exercise, the density of a dog's coat and the temperature of the environment.

The best you can do, therefore, is to follow a rough guide on quantities and trust to your common sense and watchful eye to ensure that you are feeding neither too much nor too little. Bear in mind that the young adult tends to be more active than the older dog, which in turn is more active than the aged. The working dog expends more energy than the average household pet. The puppy, however, has the highest food requirement per unit of weight of any dog and needs to be fed accordingly.

Puppy feeding

A guide to the total daily food intake of growing puppies for small, medium and larger breeds is given in Table 1. A small breed will just about treble its weight between two and four months of age. The medium-size breeds grow rather more slowly, taking another month to triple their weight, and the larger breeds need six more weeks. This growth rate demands a lot of food to support it, which is why the daily food intake of the growing pup is much higher than that of an adult of the same weight.

Table 1. A guide to total daily food intake for rearing puppies from three to five months of age for small (S), medium (M) and large (L) breeds.

Age	3 MONTHS			4 MONTHS			5 MONTHS		
Type of dog	S	M	L	S	M	L	S	M	L
Body weight (lb/*kg*)	6.5/*2.95*	15/*6.8*	25/*11.3*	8/*3.6*	19/*8.6*	35/*16*	10/*4.5*	23/*10.4*	47/*21.3*
Ration 1									
Wholemeal bread (oz/*g*)	4/*140*	9/*252*	16/*448*	5.5/*154*	10/*280*	20/*56*	6/*168*	11/*308*	22/*616*
Minced beef (oz/*g*)	6/*168*	8/*224*	16/*448*	7/*196*	10/*280*	19/*532*	7.5/*210*	12/*336*	22/*616*
Sterile bone flour (oz/*g*)	1/*28*	2/*56*	3/*84*	1/*28*	2/*56*	3/*84*	1/*28*	2/*56*	3/*84*
Cod liver oil (teaspoons)	1	1.5	2.5	1	1.5	2.5	1	1.5	2.5
Egg	1	1	2	1	1	2	1	1	2
Ration 2									
Canned dog meat (oz/*g*)	2/*56*	3.5/*98*	7/*196*	3/*84*	4.75/*133*	10/*280*	3.5/*98*	7/*196*	14/*392*
Puppy meal (oz/*g*)	6/*168*	8/*224*	14/*392*	6.5/*182*	9.5/*266*	16/*448*	7/*196*	10/*280*	18/*504*
Ration 3									
Dry dog food (complete food) (oz/*g*)	6.5/*182*	9.5/*266*	16/*448*	7.5/*210*	11/*308*	19/*532*	8/*224*	13/*364*	22/*616*

In addition, provide a daily milk ration of ¼ pint (5 fl oz) for small breeds, ½ pint (10 fl oz) for medium breeds and ¾ pint (15 fl oz) for large breeds over the three months.

Coping with a puppy's food requirements is surprisingly simple, providing you follow a few cardinal rules.

1. Assuming that your puppy is about eight weeks old on arrival, it is likely to have been fed three or four times a day. This can be reduced to a twice-daily feeding regime when it is three or four months old, each meal being equal quantities of the same food.

2. The dish should be removed after 10–15 minutes even if food remains. This trains the pup to eat what it wants while food is available and avoids the cardinal sin of eating between meals.

3. The amount of food offered must be increased as the puppy grows. Most pups are not greedy but only eat more or less what they need. Once a week offer a measured, excessive amount at each meal so that when appetite is satisfied you can measure what remains and set the amount for the following week.

The trouble is knowing whether *your* pup is greedy or not. Keep a careful eye on its progress and providing it does not start to get fat you will be able to relax. If, on the other hand, the pup starts to look like a football you should reduce the food intake, especially if it only moves when you kick it!

4. Pups can be transferred from special puppy foods on to foods prepared for adult dogs at between three and four months of age. They still need to be fed at a higher rate than the adult until the period of rapid growth is over (which is five months old for toy breeds, six months for the medium breeds and eight months for the large). By this time your puppy will be consuming about one-third more than its adult intake level. Since growth now slows down considerably, it is essential to reduce food intake rapidly to avoid obesity.

Feeding adult dogs

The adult dog needs to be fed only once a day, but owners are inclined to take an anthropomorphic approach and want to feed at least twice daily. There is no harm in this as long as the total daily intake is not increased. Small breeds may not be able to take in an adequate amount when fed only once a day, and your vet may advise more frequent feeding for any breed if the dog has a condition that requires controlled dietary intake.

A guide to the amounts to be fed are given in Table 2 for canned meat fed with biscuit meal, Table 3 for canned meat and cereal and Table 4 for both semi-moist and expanded dry dog foods – see pages 32, 33 and 34. Remember that these are only an indication of average amounts and will vary.

Myths of dog feeding

Providing your dog has a balanced diet it can be fed virtually anything; at least, as long as you are not about to start feeding powdered glass or hemlock.

There is much nonsense about dog foods uttered by those who should know better, for example idiotic statements to the effect that you should feed only raw meat to a dog because this is 'natural' and anyway what it would eat in the

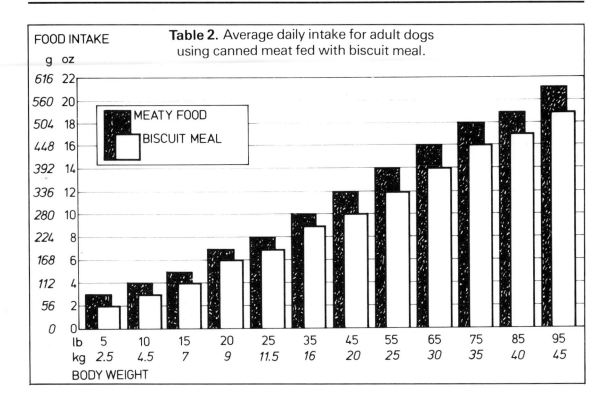

FOOD INTAKE

Table 2. Average daily intake for adult dogs using canned meat fed with biscuit meal.

MEATY FOOD
BISCUIT MEAL

BODY WEIGHT

wild. Presumably from the local butcher! But dogs are not wild, they are domesticated. Admittedly their wild ancestors ate raw meat, but what else were they supposed to do? It was man who mastered the art of cooking over a camp fire. You might as well argue that nature drove dogs to become domesticated so that they could enjoy their meat cooked!

Another fallacy is that dogs do not need vegetables because they are descended from carnivores. It is true that the wolf (the dog's closest relative and probable ancestor) is a flesh-eater, but its prey mostly consists of herbivores and the wolf eats the entrails as well as the best steaks. No doubt you are now glad that we have grocery stores.

Perhaps you think there is no harm in feeding your dog raw meat, but you should think again. Even uncooked meat from the most hygienic butcher may be covered with bacteria that can not only infect your dog and make it ill, but which can also be passed on to the family and, even worse, to you!

Bones

For the same reason, it is not advisable to feed uncooked bones to a dog. What is more, any bones that are given should be

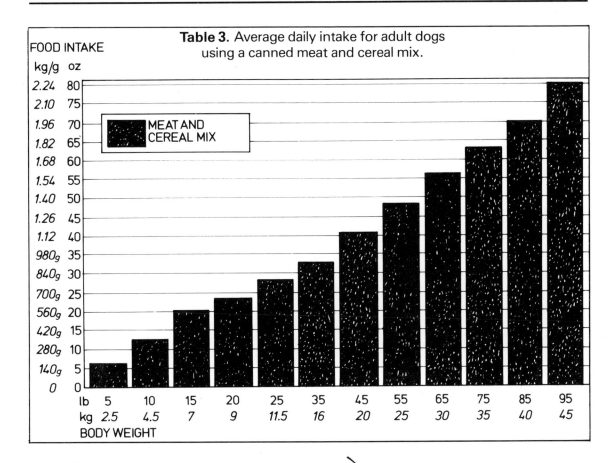

Table 3. Average daily intake for adult dogs using a canned meat and cereal mix.

FOOD INTAKE

kg/g	oz
2.24	80
2.10	75
1.96	70
1.82	65
1.68	60
1.54	55
1.40	50
1.26	45
1.12	40
980g	35
840g	30
700g	25
560g	20
420g	15
280g	10
140g	5
0	0

MEAT AND CEREAL MIX

lb	5	10	15	20	25	35	45	55	65	75	85	95
kg	2.5	4.5	7	9	11.5	16	20	25	30	35	40	45

BODY WEIGHT

beef shin-bones and no smaller, and not from any other animal – with the possible exception of an elephant. The alternative is to risk an emergency trip to the vet to have, say, a chicken leg extracted from your dog and a large sum of money extracted from you.

When the dog has eaten the marrow and the bone is starting to break up, remove it before the dog's bowel contents become rather too solid. It may not actually pass the proverbial brick but the close similarity to reinforced concrete is

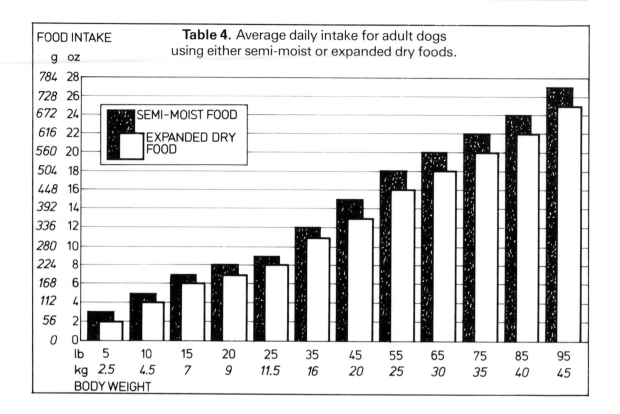

Table 4. Average daily intake for adult dogs using either semi-moist or expanded dry foods.

not very pleasant. Take care not to provoke a scene when removing the offending article as even the most chewed-over relic may be jealously defended. If in doubt, wait until Fido is taking a nap – a short game on awakening may induce him to forget about the matter entirely.

Health and beauty

It is all very well putting petrol and oil into your car but unless you are unusually dim you also ensure that if the car is not running well something is done to put it right. You will also give it the occasional spit and polish. The same applies to your dog. Just as you notice any change in the performance of your car so you will learn to spot any deviation from normal in your dog. It will take a little while to get to know what is normal, but as time goes on it becomes instinctive.

Anyone with common sense does not wait until things go seriously wrong before consulting the experts. With sufficient knowledge, of course, they can deal with minor problems themselves and, if their diagnosis is correct, save money. It must be recognized that when the big ends are going on a car it is not much good replacing the sparking plugs. It will neither cure the problem nor avert the heavy expense that is bound to ensue. It may even cost more at the end of the day. It is as well, then, to acquire some knowledge if only to know when you should seek advice. The following pages are intended to do just that. More detailed advice on particular problems and how to repair them will be found in Chapters 5, 6 and 7.

Recognizing ill health

The common changes in behaviour that would suggest your dog is ill include loss of appetite, not welcoming you when you come down first thing in the morning, diarrhoea, vomiting, increased thirst (with or without increased urine output), signs of pain, lameness, excess panting (except in very hot conditions) and any other abnormal signs you can think of!

Disease prevention

Some diseases are, or have been, serious problems to the dog breeder and owner. The same can be said of man, but with the spread of vaccination diseases such as smallpox, diphtheria, tetanus and polio are no longer the threat that they once were.

For dogs, vaccines have played a considerable part in the control of distemper, both forms of leptospirosis and, more recently, canine parvovirus infection. In those countries where rabies is rife, vaccines have been of considerable benefit in reducing the threat to the dog and, through it, to the owner.

There are some other diseases for which vaccines are available and your vet will advise you on their value. You may well meet those who doubt either the efficacy of vaccines or the need for boosters to keep the immunity up. There are even those who disapprove of vaccines because they have been developed as a result of experiments on animals, but it is difficult to justify putting millions at risk in order that a few hundred may be saved.

The other extreme view – that if a vaccine is available then it should be used by all – is more suitable for the salesman than for those who take a balanced view of their dog's best interests. But if a disease is a killer, causes serious illness or after-effects in the animal, can be passed on to man, or spreads in epidemic proportions then a vaccine is certainly justified.

There are other situations in which you can take preventive measures, for example avoiding contact with known infectious conditions such as mange and ringworm. Roundworms can be controlled effectively with preventive dosing at appropriate intervals (see Chapter 6, page 99). Although roundworms do not generally cause much problem to the dog, there are public health aspects that make it desirable to ensure they are removed.

It comes down to common sense. If you take sensible precautions, feed your dog properly, keep it clean and in dry, draught-free conditions and frequently

exercised there is every chance of trouble-free pet ownership. Just do not break mirrors or walk under ladders!

Exercise

When feeding was discussed it was pointed out that the amount of food required depends partly upon the amount of exercise a dog is given. If your bank manager suggests a period of belt tightening, make sure it is your own and not the dog's. A dog *needs* exercise for a healthy life and it costs you nothing but a little food and some shoe leather. However, do not overdo the exercise for a growing puppy. Plan its exercise so that it gets home before it is exhausted. Once fully grown and with bones well developed, dogs can stand more exercise than you can.

It is of paramount importance that your dog is kept firmly under control when taking exercise. Once you are able to take your dog outside you should keep it on a lead until it is trained to come when called. Never permit your dog to become a nuisance to others, human or animal.

Bathing

There is a popular misconception that puppies should not be bathed until they are 'old enough' or 'until they are X months old'. Thank heaven no such rumour is rife as far as babies are concerned! It is simply a matter of being sensible. Just as you would not bath a baby in a cold room, you must ensure

that a puppy is not permitted to get cold when bathing. Remember that wet hair removes the insulating effect of the fur coat it was born with.

The dog's bathwater should be luke-warm; on a fine day you can bath it out-side and save yourself the likelihood of mess inside. Use a suitable bowl or tub for the purpose, *not* the family bath if you can avoid it. There is a plethora of sham-poos available, some suitable for all breeds, some specially for dogs with long and easily tangled coats, still others in-tended to highlight coat colours or for dogs with delicate skins, such as puppies. Dry, powder shampoos are also obtain-able, together with a range of coat conditioners for the pampered pooch. However, ordinary baby shampoo will often do just as well.

Lather the dog thoroughly – not for-getting to shampoo between its toes where there are glands – and rinse with clean water. Take particular care with the head so as not to get shampoo in its eyes. Once the bath is complete, dry the coat thoroughly with warm towels and finish off with a hair dryer or, if it is a warm day, a run round the garden.

There is no definite rule for frequency of bathing: a dog should be bathed as necessary. This generally means when it is dirty or smelly, or both. One advan-tage of starting bathing early in life is that the dog gets used to it and can even learn to enjoy it. If the first bath is shallow and each succeeding one is gradually deepened, it soon becomes an accepted part of the dog's life and with any luck you will not end up the wettest participant!

Grooming

If a bath is not a daily necessity in the canine world, brushing and combing cer-tainly is. Admittedly, short-haired coats are less time consuming and require less specialist equipment, but long coats need a great deal of work and missing just one day can land you with rather more than you bargained for. Should this happen you can always take the easy way out and stroll down to your neighbourhood poodle parlour to have the job done prop-erly. That will probably give you enough financial incentive to keep to a daily routine!

Your grooming equipment should in-clude, at the least, a soft brush, a comb (preferably mounted on a handle and certainly without sharp teeth) and scissors. Many people find a grooming glove – with a 'brush' attached – a useful extra.

Stand the dog on a flat surface, preferably on newspaper, and brush from the head down and back, always following the lie of the fur. A thorough combing after brushing will remove any remaining dead hair and impart a sheen to the coat. Some breeds demand particularly close attention, especially those with feathered legs and tails; and spaniels, for example, should have the hair on their ears clipped from time to time to keep out ear infections.

A few breeds need periodic clipping in addition to brushing and combing. These include poodles and, in very hot weather, breeds such as the Old English Sheepdog. A grooming parlour is the best place – perhaps you cannot avoid one after all. However, most dogs moult quite naturally in spring and autumn and do not need their coats clipped at all – although you will probably need to be ready with the vacuum cleaner at such times.

Check your dog's feet from time to time and clip away hair that grows beyond the level of the pad, looking for any signs of cuts or inflammation while doing so. A well-exercised dog should keep its claws worn down without any help from you, but over-long claws can be painful and should be clipped back. Have the vet do this as it is most important not to cut the quick of the claw.

Eyes, ears and teeth

The occasional 'sleep' first thing in the morning in the inner corner of both eyes is quite normal and can be gently wiped away with cotton wool moistened with warm water. If the eyes need to be cleaned more frequently they should be checked by your vet.

Ears should be cleaned weekly. Use a piece of moistened cotton wool large enough not to be lost down the ear canal! A light brown wax in small quantities is normal in some ears but be suspicious of wax resembling dark tan shoe polish, especially if there is enough to clean a pair of shoes! Ear mites are the likely cause (see page 100 for how to deal with them). If the skin lining the ear and the ear canal is reddened, this is a sign of inflammation; and a discharge and/or abnormal smell could mean that you have missed the earlier stages of it. In any event get down to your vet.

Some people seem to think that only one condition affects the dog's ear – the dreaded canker. However, this is a very general expression that covers a range of ear conditions. Successful treatment depends on determining the precise cause so that appropriate action can be taken, which is why it is always important to seek professional advice for ear problems.

Dogs keep their teeth remarkably clean without the aid of toothpaste and brush. Indeed, compared to man, tooth decay is relatively rare in dogs. The biggest problem in the dog's mouth is deposits of tartar on the teeth. In most dogs this does not become an obvious problem until they are several years old, when owners usually complain about bad breath. The only answer is to scale the teeth, under a general anaesthetic. This will cause no pain to the dog, which is probably less than can be said for a visit to your own dentist, it will cost less than a shampoo and set at a poodle parlour and will be necessary far less often!

Some breeds, however, need their teeth scaled far earlier because of tartar and trapped food particles. These tend to be the toy breeds, especially those with long mouths, such as miniature and toy poodles. A small, soft toothbrush as used for babies can be used from puppyhood in such cases. They soon get used to it and accept it as a regular, if not daily, part of their grooming.

Safety

Safety in the home

For the first few weeks after its arrival, a puppy should spend part of the time confined to its own area away from the rough and tumble of the average home. This is as much for its own protection as for the owner's peace of mind. But as the puppy

grows and learns to behave itself, especially concerning what it can do and where to do it, so it will find its world growing steadily larger. In the process it also learns that the risks of injury to itself are in direct proportion to the ground area to which it is exposed. This is even before it walks near a road! Just hope that babies do not get trodden on as often as puppies.

It is as well to remember that although the dog has to adapt to life in the home, so the occupants of the home have to adapt themselves to its presence – such as learning not to kneel on the carpet without first checking it is dry. Fortunately, puppies grow or are trained out of that particular fault – but just like children, eliminate one fault and another comes along to take its place.

As a puppy grows bigger more items come within reach and, invariably, so does their value. Just when you thought it had done about as much damage as any dog could do, that family heirloom in the shape of a Ming vase finds itself at tail level and is dealt a cracking blow as you are settling down to watch the big match. As you scrabble for the pieces, at least you can console yourself with the thought that it could never have been the real thing, could it?

Nature provides a balance in all things. For every risk to your life and property there is another one to a dog's life (and property if you include some minor bits and pieces, such as its bed, collar and lead). The young dog's horizons gradually extend to include things like stairs, a hazard with great potential for enhancing the standard of living for your vet. Then, just to lull a growing puppy into a sense of false security in that haven it was used to in the kitchen, its now increased size doubles the chances of causing mishaps at the very moment when its owner has a boiling hot cup of tea in his or her hand. And the larger the dog, the greater the chance that the tea – abandoned in mid-air as you fight desperately for balance – will land all over it. At this stage you either wonder why the vet has not got a Rolls Royce or understand why he has.

Of course, real safety in the home rather depends on the kind of home you have. You are unlikely to encounter many problems in a flat or apartment, although do remember to keep that inviting window closed if it fronts a drop of 20 storeys or more! However, there are two very important aspects of safety in any home.

The first concerns electricity. Plugs, flexes and nose-high electric fittings generally can appear interestingly playful to the young dog, particularly those flexes that snake around a room. Never leave a flex lying around or a live fitting switched on where a pup can get at it, and firmly discourage any signs of interest in them.

The second concerns poisons. These include not only the obviously dangerous compounds that you might use in the garden or to control pests, but a whole range of household products – bleaches and disinfectants, paints, polishes, antifreeze for the car and so on. Some houseplants are poisonous to dogs – as they are to humans – and, finally, there are all the tasty alcoholic beverages in the drinks cabinet and kitchen. Keep *anything* that

may damage your dog well out of sight, preferably in a paw-proof cabinet, or at least out of reach in the case of houseplants and the like. If your dog does manage to eat or drink something dangerous, turn to page 109 for advice on emergency first aid.

Safety in the car

In many cases the puppy met the car on the same day it met its owners. That may or may not have been a pleasurable experience (meeting the car, that is). It possibly depended on whether the puppy was sick or not (which in turn influences *your* degree of pleasure).

Opposite: *Mild, affectionate and quite unmistakable, the Basset Hound is one of the most warmly regarded breeds.*

Opposite above: *Boxers can appear rather disciplinarian as parents, but the breed makes an affectionate family pet.*

Opposite below: *Not many Standard Poodles miss a chance to pose for the camera, even if the rest of the family has other ideas.*

Above: *Mealtime for a litter of Golden Retriever pups – but do make sure that Mum gets enough, too.*

The second experience of travelling by car is usually a visit to the vet. It need not be an unpleasant experience as most injections can be virtually painless. However, the fact is that some dogs love cars and others find them the equivalent of a mobile Hole of Calcutta.

It is a good plan to introduce a puppy to your car early on, so that the car is regarded more as an extension to the home than as a noisy, smelly conveyance. Give it the occasional meal in the car, let it play in the car, even sleep in the car, but do not move the car an inch.

Encourage the puppy to regard the car as something enjoyable, though not to the extent of treating the gear stick as a bone. When vaccinations are complete and the day comes for a walk outside, drive with the pup to the nearest park or open space. In this way it will look upon trips in the car with anticipation rather than foreboding.

Safety in the garden

With two exceptions, it is the dog that should adapt to the garden and not vice versa. The first is making the garden dog-proof – and the garden should be dog-proof to keep *your* dog IN and *other* dogs OUT. This is particularly important if you have a bitch that is neither spayed nor on the pill. In this respect, then, the garden must be adapted to the dog.

The second adaptation of the garden to the dog relates to how you handle toxic chemicals in the form of weedkillers and so on. Recognizing that the garden can be entered by wildlife and cats, you will have been somewhat careful about the way you spread them around before. Now be twice as careful. The first step along that path is to read the labels carefully, twice, and not leave anything where an inquisitive dog can get at it.

It has been assumed that your garden is a model of horticultural elegance and perfection. If that assumption was an error of judgement and your garden is

Opposite: Two Wire-haired Dachshund puppies. Dachsunds make ideal pets and adapt well to towns. Go easy with the dog food, however.

what might be described tactfully as *au naturel*, then a third adaptation is required. Remove all pieces of broken glass, old cans, bones and other dangerous items before you let the dog out. Now it is all plain sailing, simply the adaptation of the puppy to the garden.

At least there should be no problem in getting the puppy out there. The problem is to get it to stay in the right parts. Restrict it to paths (if you have them) initially, then to the grass (if you have it) and finally keep it off the flower-beds. If you have none of those either, then your garden is truly *au naturel* and no adaptation will be required at all. However, start out the way you mean to go on. Training a dog to keep to the paths and not to make messes on the lawn (which will otherwise become dotted with little yellow patches) not only makes for good hygiene at home but discourages such activity in public parks, especially in children's play areas.

The outside world

If the general plan was to adapt the dog to the garden rather than the other way round (with the exception of a couple of areas within your control), there is no alternative for the outside world. It has to be adaptation.

There is no doubt that a substantial number of people, particularly in urban areas, resent the presence of dogs around them. In some cases this is due to a genuine fear of dogs – and a few owners do allow attack-trained monsters to roam in public places – in others to a not unreasonable objection to the fouling of pavements. However, an even greater number of people resent the presence of those who wish to ban dogs altogether. If all owners rose to their responsibilities and ensured that public parks and streets were kept clean, wholesome and free from canine excrement there is no doubt that anti-dog campaigners would have very much less to complain about.

Every owner should appreciate that the general public have the right to walk in public places without fear for themselves or their own pets. This means that every owner who takes a dog into public places *must* have it under control, with or without a lead – and preferably with one. Even if your dog is normally well behaved you should always carry a lead just in case of emergency – if only because it was you that was hit by the bus and somebody has to get the dog home.

Dogs should never be let out on the streets or in parks unaccompanied. It is possible for a dog to escape, of course, but in that event it should be wearing a collar with the owner's name and address or telephone number, and preferably with the vet's telephone number engraved on the reverse of the disc for use in the event of an accident.

Canine behaviour can be antisocial to other dogs, not only to other people. Other dogs have the right to walk the streets, and fights should never arise in the presence of owners. Indeed, in this respect they should never arise at all.

3. Conquering canine cunning

Over the past 30 years, a multiplicity of 'new' disciplines for formal study have been developed, covering any number of different aspects of our daily lives. In fact most of these are far from new, only the formal assembly of much that was already known and applied in the everyday lives of salesmen, businessmen and so forth.

The study of animal behaviour, otherwise known as ethology, has its roots in the thousands of years of association between man and his fellow animals. We have been conditioned into thinking that man is superior to other animals because of his ability to do many things that they cannot, but it is as well to remember that

1. We are not superior in everything we do.

2. We are also animals, just another species in fact.

3. We have to adjust to live with other animals (including fellow men).

4. We have to learn in order to teach.

Those running successful small business operations do not *have* to attend courses on personnel management to be good employers, but some knowledge of human behaviour and their needs helps in the management of employees.

If you are to manage your dog so that it satisfies your demands on it and is in turn happy with its lot and wants to stay with you (and, of course, you want to keep it), you must have some idea of what you are doing. Forget about following your own instincts: instead, work upon the dog's instincts and turn them to your advantage.

Canine behaviour

The dog is a pack animal. It is by nature gregarious but wants to be top of the heap; in other words, it is much like us humans. And it is instinct, from the outset, that is the real driving force of a dog's activity. Fortunately, instinctive behaviour can be overcome by what is termed acquired or conditioned behaviour. It is fortunate because otherwise there would be too many chiefs and not enough indians, in both canine and human society.

One can see in both those worlds the individuals who have come out on top, those who are not yet on top but intend to be and those who accept their position in the hierarchy. This can be seen in schools (and not only at the pupil level!), offices and factories, in the armed forces and even in the home. Who wears the trousers in your home? You need not answer that, just make sure it is not the dog!

This is the basic principle behind all attempts to conquer canine cunning. Your new pup may well have learned that it is not destined for Prime Minister or President before it leaves its mother, but do not count on it. Remember that there are those in your own circle who think they should be running the show. Even if they are clearly never going to

succeed, they can cause plenty of confusion in their attempts to do so. Never allow your dog to think that anyone but you is in charge.

Body language

Body language is demonstrated by most members of the animal kingdom, but each species has its own displays and interpretations of them. An example is the friendly wagging tail of the dog, behaviour that denotes displeasure in the cat.

Dogs are not unlike humans in that they communicate their feelings to one another through eyes, ears, mouth, lips and body posture. In the absence of spontaneous reaction, such as aggression or invitation to play, the usual activity is mutual investigation, initially nose to nose, and then nose to each other's scent glands under the tail.

Submissive behaviour

The submissive dog holds its ears back and flat, close to the head, adopts a crouching position on all four legs and keeps its head and tail pointing downwards. Under real pressure, the act of submission can progress to the dog rolling on one side and thus explosing its belly, the sign of complete submission. Any resemblance to similar behaviour in humans is purely coincidental!

This attitude may be adopted when the dog has misbehaved and is either scolded by the owner or even when no words have been expressed at all – an angry look, for example. Just as you learn to read a dog's behaviour so it learns *your* reactions. It is often interpreted as cowering but is, in fact, submission.

Inviting play

When soliciting play the dog holds its tail high and extends the front legs forwards, thus lowering its front while keeping the back end raised. This is usually followed by 'paddling' with the front paws and perhaps even a little prancing about, followed by the adoption of the first posture again. There could be some gentle barking, all designed to persuade the individual to whom the behaviour is directed to play.

Aggressive behaviour

Both aggression and fear are shown by the dog making itself appear as large as possible. The aggressive dog stands to its full height, hackles raised and tail up. If the ears are capable of standing up, they are erect. The eyes stare at the opponent and the teeth are bared. Watch out!

Fear

The dog showing fear, on the other hand, although standing erect, leans backwards with its hackles up and ears pressed back close to the head. The tail is held low, sometimes even between the legs, and the teeth are bared. The posture is not dissimilar to that of the aggressive dog but is quite easily distinguished. Just call its bluff. If it was fear, the dog will back down. If it was aggression, you should back down.

Eye-to-eye confrontation

The eyes play a very important part in body language between dog and dog, and even between dog and man (or vice versa). A stare from a dominant dog to a submissive one maintains the dominant dog's position in the hierarchy. If there is any doubt about relative dominance, that stare is an overture to a fight.

If a human stares at a dog it will usually respond with submission and look away. There are some dogs that express fear mixed with a little bravado, giving the odd bark. Turn yourself away from such dogs so that your eyes do not meet and they will generally come up and smell your legs, and even an outstretched hand. As soon as your eyes meet again, they will back off.

If you stare at an extremely dominant and aggressive dog you may provoke an attack, so watch out. Or, rather, watch the dog, but do not look it in the eye!

Hunting instincts

Being carnivorous, a dog will chase prey instinctively although the instinct may not be as well developed in urban environments. First there is the lack of opportunity and second there is not a great deal of incentive when the terms are full board! Not that all hunting is for food to meet immediate requirements. In towns there is little to chase but cats and squirrels and that is usually fruitless.

On the other hand, a dog that has been brought up with cats may never chase them, in much the same way as it may not spend its time chasing people; at

least, not without provocation. This is an acquired behaviour pattern through awareness that its home is also occupied by others. The behaviour may also have been acquired through unpleasant experiences with cats in the past.

Take your dog to the country, however, and it may be a different matter. The worrying of livestock – in Britain the usual victims are sheep – is almost always disastrous and you should assume that your dog will do so until you can be certain that it will not. This is, first, to avoid damage to the livestock and second to avoid your dog being chased by an irate farmer with a loaded gun, a drastic but legal remedy on his part in most countries. He has a right to protect his property and your dog will have an instinct to protect yours.

Territory

Territorial defence is usually the prerogative of the pack leader. We hope by now that you have established yourself in that role (unless you have taught your dog to read and it is the dog's turn to read this book).

Your dog will regard other dogs and even humans entering your property as a threat to its territory unless experience has indicated that they are welcomed by the owner, especially a dominant owner. The dominant owner is the pack leader who, as indicated earlier, has the post of Defence Secretary and Prime Minister or President rolled into one. As long as the owner is not aggressive to visitors, why should the dog be? This explains why so many people think their pet will be useless as a watchdog – and yet, if the owner is absent, any visitor is made distinctly unwelcome.

Now all you need to do is look around your dog-owning friends and determine how their dog reacts to visitors in front of its owners. You will soon discover who is the real pack leader in a particular household!

Conditioned behaviour

Anybody with any interest in animals is likely to have heard of Pavlov's experiments and the 'conditioned reflex' in dogs (and, indeed, in other animals). Pavlov demonstrated in his classic studies in animal behaviour that if a bell was rung every time he fed his dogs, a time would come when ringing the bell *without offering food* would be followed by salivation.

Salivation is not something that is under voluntary control, even in man; you cannot turn the flow of saliva on at will. It is possible, of course, to imagine something appetizing and thereby stimulate the flow of saliva, but that is still a reflex action. Although that may be the case in man, it is doubtful whether a dog can imagine a tasty meal in the same way. Instead, a dog fed at regular times can develop a conditioned reflex and start to salivate automatically at such times even if food is not offered, providing the dog has a good internal clock.

Instinctive behaviour can be conditioned in much the same way. This is a principle used in all training. It may be achieved by making the dog realize that a desire to empty bladder and bowels is associated with being placed in your chosen spot for this activity, or by the association of a word of command with some action you wish the dog to take, especially if this is reinforced by reward.

It is easily seen, therefore, that the behavioural patterns of your dog can be conditioned and used to your advantage. It must not be forgotten, of course, that carelessness might also unwittingly condition your dog to behave in an undesirable way, and then you will have all the fun of trying to decondition it. By that time, no doubt, you will regard Pavlov as mere child's play.

Canine intelligence

The question of whether animals are capable of independent thought, in the way that humans are, has long been of abiding interest to scientists, philosophers and wiseacres of every kind. It sounds distinctly fanciful – you can hardly ask an animal's opinion – though many owners are convinced that their dog has shown flashes of inspiration and

may even observe that 'it understands every word I say'.

The question really comes down to whether an animal is capable of interpreting its experience to reach conclusions that it did not know before, or whether it reacts to life as a simple matter of cause and effect. There is no doubt that some dogs learn faster than others and, one suspects, desire to learn faster than others. Whether this is a matter of intelligence or a greater desire to please the owner is a moot point. Some feats may even be accomplished for self-gratification, such as opening the door of the refrigerator. It may well be as a result of observing the owner doing so, combined with the knowledge that the fridge contains food. Perhaps that was a reasoning process? Or simply an associative one, connecting food with an open door? Or was it only an accidental discovery?

It does not really matter. There is little point in arguing with the owner who proudly claims mental prowess for Fido that rivals that of Einstein – far better to point out that dogs take after their owners and thereby confirm how perceptive you are. If your own dog is a little slow, however, it is better to avoid that response and mutter something about genetics and inherited genius.

Inherited intelligence

There is clear evidence of differences in intelligence between littermates, between strains within breeds and even between breeds. Where there are restricted numbers of a breed available for mating it is inevitable that there will be a certain amount of inbreeding, but providing this is not overdone there is no deleterious effect upon intelligence.

The vast majority of breeders have the interests of the breed uppermost in their minds and adopt a responsible attitude in selection of sires for their breeding bitches. Unfortunately, a minority are more interested in mass production of puppies at the lowest possible cost with a view to maximizing profit. Breeds that have become too popular too quickly, such as the Cocker Spaniel, Corgi and Old English Sheepdog, therefore have *some* strains which have been too closely bred, with a consequent deterioration of appearance, temperament and intelligence.

Some breeds have been trained to carry out specific functions over hundreds of successive generations and those qualities rendering them most suitable for the purpose have now been inbred. Gundogs, for example, have to be unperturbed by the sound of gunfire, not move until told, have a soft mouth and not eat the bag. Naturally, only the best gundogs tend to be used for breeding and as a result working strains of gundogs almost invariably have the perfect temperament and intelligence for the purpose and are easily trained. In that sense, their intelligence is inherited.

Developing intelligence

To make the most of intelligence, man has devised formal systems of learning in all civilized societies. There are, of course, those rare specimens whose innate genius is demonstrated at an early age. Most of us show aptitude for something before embarking on formal education but have to learn to realize the potential of the brain power with which we were endowed.

This is the process of developing our innate intelligence. It comes easier to some than to others. Dogs are much the same. They learn from experience from an early age; some learn quicker than others. Those learning processes inevitably stimulate the canine mind to apply itself, whether it be instinctive or conditioned behaviour. Just how far that development can go depends on the ability of the dog, in the same way that not all children benefit to the same extent from school.

So much depends on the pupil, teacher and owners (or parents?) who are all interactive. If the pupil has respect for the other members of the triangle it will want to please them. Your dog will want to please you, so use that desire to your own ends. It will make your life and that of your pet so much more enjoyable.

Early training

You cannot start training too early in life, whether you are man or beast. It may be only the simplest of things that are learned at first, but your puppy will already have been taught the rudiments by its mother prior to purchase. The standards a mother desires may well differ from yours but, in any case, there is every reason for you to aspire to greater heights than she. You, in turn, will have every hope that the pup will aspire to greater heights too!

Punishment or reward?

It has been pointed out earlier that rearing children is very similar to the rearing of puppies. Wives tend to put it the other way: rearing puppies is like rearing children. Nowadays, it is the vogue to let children do more or less what they like so that they develop their own characters, although fortunately as not every parent subscribes to this view there are still some lovable children about. If you have an *avant garde* approach to child rearing, either become a disciplinarian with the dog or pass it on to a more suitable home before any harm is done to it. Firm control is *essential*. This does not mean, however, that sparing the rod spoils the dog any more than it spoils the child.

Conditioning behaviour to conform with your wishes is achieved more easily and quickly by rewarding success rather than by punishing failure. There may be times when punishment is justified, but never let it be in anger. If you cannot control *yourself*, how can you expect your puppy to do so?

Punishment must be immediate if it is to be used at all, which does not mean immediately you discover the puppy has been naughty but immediately following the *act*. It is only then that the puppy can associate the punishment with the offence that has annoyed you. If it associates the punishment with something acceptable to you, it is going to become terribly confused, and especially so if the act happens to be one that may otherwise have been rewarded from time to time.

Punishment should be limited to a tap on the backside, at the most. The purpose is to indicate disapproval, never to inflict pain. Small dogs may be held by the scruff of the neck and shaken gently. At the same time, express your feelings by using the command (such as 'bad dog') that you have decided to apply to the pup whenever you are displeased, without upsetting any passing mother with young children.

It is far better to concentrate on reward. Again this should be immediate in order that the pup associates it with the act that delighted you. Remember that a dog loves to please its owner, although do not reward with titbits *every* time the pup performs or the good pupil will very quickly become a fat one. However, it will need enough titbits to learn that the gentle 'good boy' and the pat on the head

that accompanies them are, in themselves, a reward. So if it is a little slow in learning, go back over earlier lessons until you obtain the desired results. Eventually, verbal approval will be just as effective as oral reward.

Words of command

Words of command must be chosen before training starts. It does not really matter what the words are providing they are distinct, cannot be confused with any other command and are said in a standard way. About half a dozen will suffice for most owners.

Even if the dog has difficulty in grasping what you want it to do, do not get exasperated and raise your vocal tone or pitch as you repeat the command yet again. It will only confuse the dog and increase your exasperation.

The trainer

In a family there is bound to be interest in the puppy from most, if not all, members of the household. They will all want to contribute to its education but not, one hopes, to its training. Only one member of the household should be responsible for that, for all training must be organized, consistent and move on to the next stage only when the previous one has been thoroughly learned. Earlier lessons should also be repeated from time to time to ensure that they have not been forgotten.

This task needs someone who is around daily and has the time to devote to it, although it is not essential to train at a fixed time every day. Indeed, there is a danger in training at a fixed time because the puppy may decide that it need be on its best behaviour only during its regular lesson.

Once training is complete, a dog should know the commands well enough not to be confused by hearing them uttered in a different tone or pitch. This means that other members of the household can now use them with fair hope of success, unless your spouse speaks English with a Serbo-Croat twang.

Duration of training

At first a young puppy will concentrate for only a few minutes at a time, but before long it will take ten minutes in its stride. The important thing is to catch the signs of flagging interest. A lesson must not become a bore (for dog or trainer) nor a game, although it must be enjoyable (for both). As the puppy reaches five to six months of age it will

put up with 20 minutes at either end of the day as part of its daily exercise.

Training adult dogs

Owners who have taken on an adult dog may be lucky and find its training is impeccable. And it is far easier if you know the previous owner and can establish the words of command that the dog is accustomed to – and how often it is accustomed to ignoring them.

Unfortunately, adult dogs obtained via homes for strays have neither name nor examination certificates. This means that to begin with you will have to experiment with a range of common names – Spot, Blackie, Patch and so on – in the hope that you will strike lucky and elicit the desired response. Just pray that the former owners were not too original and did not pick an outlandish name like Montmorency. Fortunately, words of command for the common actions one expects of the obedient dog are fairly

standard, although this is not necessarily so as the previous owners might not have been English-speaking. If your dog does not respond to 'heel' or 'sit' (these are useful to start with), undertaking a Berlitz in a number of foreign languages is not advised as it is possible the dog was not trained to any extent at all.

Training classes

Various training classes are available to owners, usually run by local canine societies. Your veterinary surgeon will know of the nearest one to your home – not that the nearest is necessarily the best. Most training classes are designed for owners of a responsible age and puppies over six months old. It is not only *dogs* that benefit from the classes!

There is also an increasing number of courses run for younger puppies that have completed their vaccinations and so are able to mix with other dogs. This is particularly useful where it is not only the puppy that is the novice, as embarrassing mistakes can be explained away on the grounds that 'he is really far too young for this kind of thing'.

Training equipment

During initial training your dog must, of course, be kept under control. This requires a collar and lead, with the puppy at one end and the owner at the other. Make quite sure that the puppy is at the right end, where the lessons are learned! Although an ordinary collar *can* be adequate, a choke collar will help more in establishing control and getting the message over to your dog. Choke collars are available in leather and nylon, but chain-link collars are to be preferred. They should be large enough to slip over the dog's head with ease but with about 1½–2 in (4–5 cm) of slack at the most when around the neck.

There is a right and a wrong way to fit a choke chain. If the dog is to walk on your left, the end of the chain attached to the lead will be on the dog's right. The chain must pass through the ring at the other end, *across* the top of the neck, down the *left* side of the dog's neck, under the jaw and up the right side. As a result, when the dog pulls ahead it tightens the collar. When it stops pulling, the lead slackens and the choke chain relaxes its grip, *as long as it was fitted correctly*.

A useful additional piece of equipment is a training lead, about 30–45 ft (9–14 m) long. This may be of nylon cord, but some excellent retractable nylon tape leads are available which allow you to extend the lead, as required, and take up any slack by depressing a button.

Basic training

It is absolutely essential to have a clear grasp of the objectives of your training programme. As the man said: 'If you do not know where you want to go, any map will serve to get you there.'

The first objectives are to get the puppy house-trained, used to a collar and lead, and sitting on command. All this should be possible by the time the vaccination programme is completed and the puppy allowed to go out. If you have a large enough garden you may also have managed to start training the pup to walk to heel on the lead. It all depends on how much time you have and how quickly your dog learns.

However, bear in mind the golden rule of training: teach one step at a time and only move on to the next one when the current lesson is well established. The next few pages outline the procedure for the common actions that owners should expect their dogs to perform.

House-training

If it is possible to restrict the puppy to a penned area for the first few days after its arrival you will avoid encouraging it to regard everywhere but its own bed as a lavatory. Its mother will already have taught it to keep its bed clean. Covering the pen floor with old newspapers (until it reads it will not tell the difference) and praising the pup's predictable performance on paper will establish a habit (making a firm imprint as it were!) of using the media in a way that some public figures might wish to emulate. (The implication that dogs might possibly learn to read is, of course, not true. You must therefore remember not to let today's paper slip on to the floor when relaxing in your rare moments of leisure!)

If you cannot provide a penned area the puppy will have to learn by experience where its sanitary stations are. Whenever you see that it is about to relieve itself, hastily place it on the nearest newspaper – you should already have placed several in strategic places around the house.

Once the puppy has got the message and uses the papers voluntary, whether in a penned area or not, give praise by saying 'clean boy' or 'be clean', as you choose. This is handy for kerb-training later. If caught performing off the paper around the house, scold gently and put it on the chosen place. Remember that pups tend to return and use those places they have soiled before unless the site is thoroughly cleaned and sprayed with a deodorant. For urine, one of the best agents is tonic water (without the gin). When the puppy is using the papers every time, reduce the number of sites gradually until there is only one. Ideally, this should be near the back door so that on fine days the paper can be set outside the house (let the pup watch you doing so) and once the pup is used to that site you are home and dry, and so are your carpets.

The final site outside should be chosen so that it does not become a hazard in the dark, can be cleaned up easily and is not a children's play area. Flower-beds are ideal for the purpose.

Remember that puppies frequently empty bowels and bladder in the first half hour after feeding. Keep an eye open for the imminent voiding of both in order to ensure that things are deposited on the paper before it is too late.

Training to sit

As was observed earlier, this task is often accomplished before the puppy has completed its vaccination programme and is able to walk out.

It is best to give the first few lessons when the pup's natural exuberance is flagging but before it is so weary that all it wants to do is sleep. Place a hand firmly on the hindquarters and press gently downwards as you command 'sit!'. If the dog actually sits down you have given the lesson and probably astonished both yourself and the dog. Repeat it in short sessions several times a day. Sooner or later, you will have to exert less pressure to get the pup into a sedentary position and eventually it will do so without manual contact, or so you hope. The lesson may be reinforced by giving the command 'sit!' when the dog does so of its own accord.

The next step is to extend the principle to sitting down when walking on the lead, assuming the puppy has accepted the collar and lead by now. In this case, on the command 'sit!', you bend down to put the hand on the rump, as before. The pressure on the hindquarters is reinforced by keeping the lead taut in an upwards direction. Keep the lead taut as you slowly unbend and then gradually reduce the tension as the dog sits down. Then slacken the lead and praise the dog. If it has taken hours of training to get this far and the lesson is now firmly entrenched, praise the Lord as well!

It has been stressed earlier that words of command must be expressed clearly and firmly. 'Sit!' is the one command, above all, where that injunction cannot be overemphasized. This is particularly important if you are in a public place, or in mixed company and have taken in rather more alcohol than is good for your diction.

Training to heel

A sign of a well-behaved dog, or a good owner, is the way a dog walks with you when it is on the lead (or off the lead if it is not being allowed freedom to roam around). When you start walking your dog on the lead, ensure that it is not allowed to pull ahead. Start out by saying its name and 'heel!'. If the dog pulls in front, give a sharp tug on the lead and repeat the command 'heel!' as you do so. This will check the dog and bring it back to heel. Give praise, as usual, when you get the desired response. Eventually it will become a habit.

Training to stay

Just as it is desirable to have your dog walk to heel when you take it out, there are times when you will not want it to behave as if it were your shadow when you have told it to sit.

This is where your long training lead comes into its own. Starting with the dog on your left, command it to sit. When it has done so, command 'stay!' and then slowly move in front. Again command 'stay!' and return after some seconds. If the dog has not moved, give praise and repeat the exercise. In subsequent lessons gradually increase the distance until there is implicit obedience and the dog can be literally left on its own. The same procedure can be adopted with the dog in the 'down' position (see below), as well as the 'sit'.

Training to wait and recall

There are those who substitute 'stay!' for 'wait!' in this procedure as the two are very similar. However, 'stay' is best reserved for a situation where the reunion is going to be on *your* return whereas the 'wait' is followed by your calling the dog to you.

Have the dog on the training lead sitting at your left, and with an open hand in front of its head command 'wait!'. Keeping the hand outstretched, move slowly round to the front repeating the command. Back away with the hand still out, letting out more of the lead as you go. The recall is achieved by calling the dog by name, followed by 'come!'. If there is no response, repeat the order with a slight tug of the lead as you do so; the lead should be taken in as the dog comes towards you.

In the early stages of training you should increase the distance between yourself and the dog gradually. Later, you will be able to put a fair distance between you without the dog moving. As it approaches, point out where it should stop near your feet and on reaching that position give the command 'sit!'.

Training to lie down

Start with the dog sitting on your left with a short lead in your right hand. Give the command 'down!' and at the same time bend down, pulling the lead down to the ground and so drawing the dog's neck downwards. This encourages it to lie down. If it is reluctant to do so, put two or three fingers in the collar and drag down at the same time as you pull on the lead. Should that also fail, apply gentle pressure on the neck with your left hand. As with the other commands, repeat from time to time until the lesson is well established.

Kerb-training

When out on the streets with your dog it is your responsibility to leave the pavements as clean as you found them. Even if they are less than perfect it is irresponsible to add to the mess left by others.

Having trained your dog to regard 'be clean' or another chosen expression as a word of praise, you can now convert it to a command. Whenever it is about to squat for defecation, move it towards the kerb. Providing the traffic allows, guide it into the gutter and give the command.

If there *is* heavy traffic, however, do not go near the gutter and thereby encourage the dog to perform. Even if the dog were not hit by a passing juggernaut, the probability is that the command would be superfluous!

Obedience-training

The training techniques outlined so far will make your dog an obedient member of the family. However, some owners are not satisfied with that and plunge into the advanced level course leading to entering competitions. The local dog training club will be able to help if you are interested. Obedience champion-ships tend to be dominated by the Border Collie, although German Shepherds also figure prominently among the prize winners. From here it is but a short step to training for shows, which can be a demanding affair for the medal seeker – and dog. See page 130 for more details.

The canine senses

The dog's senses are in some respects very much more acute than our own. They are also rather difficult to assess as you can hardly ask a dog what it thinks of the view, for example. Here we will con-centrate on the senses most important to you, the owner. You will already know something about your dog's sense of taste by the alacrity – or not – with which it eats its food. You will also know that it likes to be stroked and tickled, although a dog is not so constructed that it can use its sense of touch to manipulate objects in the way we can – which, perhaps, is just as well.

Smell

Smell is the most highly developed of all the canine senses. It is probably used more than sight or hearing and in some breeds this is particularly so. The hounds are prime examples. When a hound gets its nose on a scent it can be hell's own job to get its mind off it to concentrate on your commands.

All dogs use their sense of smell in everyday life. Greeting other dogs in-volves an initial nose-to-nose contact, followed by mutual investigation of the other's anal glands. Dogs mark all avail-able trees and lamp-posts with urine once they have reached sexual maturity. This is to advertise their presence to other dogs and indicates a territorial claim. The competition does not usually appear very impressed and promptly superimposes its own trade mark.

Bitches produce their own special scents when they come into heat. Phero-mones, as those substances are called, arouse sexual desire in mature male dogs. It is well known that some dogs can detect a bitch in heat at a considerable distance when upwind.

There are times when one is grateful for man's inferior sense of smell and others when it would be very convenient to be able to find one's way home without having to ask a policeman the way.

Hearing

The dog's sense of hearing, like that of smell, is infinitely superior to that of man. Although it is comparable to man's at the lower frequencies, a dog's hearing becomes more acute as the frequencies increase. The newborn pup, however, cannot hear a thing: it is born both blind and deaf, and only starts to be aware of sound after about ten days.

The dog can hear sounds from four times further away than man and within a range of between 20 and 30 000 cycles per second. In contrast we can manage a range of only 20 to 20 000 cycles. Obviously, this means that a dog can hear sounds we miss because they are beyond our range both in pitch and distance. There is one advantage to this in that high-pitched dog whistles, which are virtually inaudible to the human ear, can be picked up a considerable distance away – and the owner who uses one thereby avoids either becoming hoarse or sounding like the referee at a football match.

There is variation in hearing ability between individuals and between breeds. Prick-eared dogs usually hear better than those with drop ears, and those with larger erect ears better than those with smaller.

Sight

In some ways, man's sight is superior to that of the dog. It all depends on what the purpose of sight is. If it is important for survival in the wild to see in the dark, the dog would surpass us. If it is useful to judge distance, man surpasses the dog. If it is useful to have greater lateral vision, the dog wins.

A dog mainly detects movement, although even the sharpest-eyed specimen cannot see further than about a mile. And as the dog's ancestors evolved as hunters, with eyes placed to the side of the head, a dog can detect things moving over a much wider field of view than we can – our eyes face forwards. It did not take *our* ancestors long to realize that the dog's specialized vision and acute sense of smell, coupled with good old human cunning, would provide a formidable hunting combination. From that, perhaps, domestication began.

It used to be thought that dogs could see only in black and white. However, the structure of the canine eye suggests that they can detect colour, although not over such a wide spectrum as man. As they evolved as hunters, where the detection of movement is of prime importance, dogs have simply never needed well-developed colour vision. However, they can see in the dark much better than us. The cells in their eyes that record in black and white are more sensitive to light of low intensity and they have more of them. Anyway, if you were a dog, which would you prefer – colour television or a good meal?

4. Holidays

Believe it or not, there are pet owners who decide that they will have to part with their pet – permanently – when their annual holiday looms up. The dog was probably bought on the spur of the moment or arrived as an unwanted Christmas present. Now that an agreeable jaunt to foreign climes is on the horizon, they discover how much it costs to board a dog in kennels for the duration of the holiday, and panic.

It may even be that such owners have reared an unmanageable canine recidivist that could not be given away, even temporarily, for love or money. The holiday may be used as an excuse to salve their conscience (if they have one). At the other extreme, there are those who will not take any holiday without being able to take their pet with them.

Holidays abroad

A few countries (including Britain) have the advantage of being free of rabies. That is good news; now the bad news. In

order to preserve that enviable freedom, there are laws in rabies-free countries which restrict the import of dogs (and other animals) unless under an import licence. In Britain, such imports have to undergo six months quarantine in approved kennels. This effectively rules out taking your dog abroad on holiday, especially if the plan was to avoid leaving it in the local boarding kennels!

European and most other caninophiles, on the other hand, can cross frontiers with any pet providing they have an up-to-date certificate of vaccination against rabies. That is their good news. Their bad news is that they run the risk of catching rabies if bitten by an infected animal.

Quarantine restrictions are always strict. In a rabies-free country such as Britain, a dog is not even allowed to remain on board ship at the quayside. The moment it docks, the dog *has* to be taken to the isolation kennels. If you are planning any sea-faring adventures, therefore, it is as well to make sure that the ship does not put into the wrong port,

lest the dog is either quarantined there and then or on your return home. This might not ruin the dog, but it will most certainly ruin your holiday.

Perhaps it is safer to consider kennels for your dog, whatever your plans. The pleasures and perils of that option are discussed on pages 67–9.

Holidays at home

The term 'holidays at home' is used in the sense of 'home' rather than 'abroad', not that there is anything actually *wrong* with holidays at home. You can be bored there as easily as you can be elsewhere, but more cheaply. However, if you are really averse to the prospect of your pet being confined to a boarding kennels, you will opt for holidays at home.

This does not mean you cannot go away at all, as there are still many places that permit dogs to accompany their owner. There may be limits on size and

where a dog can go in order to avoid nuisance to other guests. In addition, you may have to pay a deposit to cover the possible damage caused by deposits from your pet!

Although bed-and-breakfast places may not exactly encourage you to bring your dog with you, especially if there is one in the house already, some hotels and caravan sites are prepared to accept them. It is vital that this is arranged when you book the accommodation and confirmed in writing in order to avoid any disappointment on arrival for your sunshine idyll. Do remember that your pet is not necessarily as lovable to other guests as it is to you, so keep it firmly under control. Strange surroundings and the close proximity of other guests may prompt boisterous or erratic behaviour, and you do not want the dog to end up in a kennels while you end up in the dog-house.

Taking your dog with you

Going on holiday means travel. This may not be easy, as it all depends on how you go. There is one advantage to a walking holiday in that travel sickness is unlikely to spoil the holiday for your dog. You may not find it all a ball of fun but whose holiday is it, anyway?

Travel by public transport is not to be recommended, unless your dog is small enough to sit on your lap. Somewhat better, perhaps, if it were small enough to fit in a capacious pocket or even a suitable piece of luggage so that you do not have to pay its fare! In any event, check with the transport company about their regulations. It is not always possible to travel by the chosen route with a dog, especially at peak travel times.

There is no doubt that the ideal means of travelling with your pet is by car. Your dog may not think so, but any embarrassment as a result of vomiting is restricted to you and your family rather than extended to the general public. And besides, it is easier to organize bladder emptying on a car journey.

One little word of advice to dog owners travelling by car with young children. It is a near certainty that a dog will perform when you stop for the kids to empty their bladders, but if you do it the other way round you can bet your life that the kids will not want to go until a little further along the road, probably just after you have passed a long line of slow-moving lorries which had been holding you up.

No doubt you restrict the fluid intake of your children before you leave and, possibly, during the journey. This can equally well be applied to your dog, within reason. You do not, or should not, restrict it completely but only in so far as it avoids rapid overflow to the bladder. A journey of over four hours should include a break for stretching the legs and light refreshment anyway, although this does involve the risk that the canine refreshment, at least, may be regurgitated before you reach your destination.

However you decide to travel, it is vital that your dog is fit before starting any journey, but more especially on public transport. If urination on a bus were embarrassing just think of the devastating effects of diarrhoea!

Motion sickness

A dog that is sick every time it goes for a trip in the car is about as happy as its owners. Some dogs are so nervous about the experience that it is almost a conditioned behaviour to start vomiting when the car moves off. More usually it is delayed just long enough to coincide with a critical motoring manoeuvre involving the outside traffic lanes. This results in frantic appeals to move to the nearside lanes so that the passenger nearest to the offending hound can gasp for air out of the window before changing into some dry clothing and discarding the vomit in a convenient gutter.

Some dogs may be less severely affected and merely salivate, albeit copiously – so copiously that you may be tempted to drill drain holes in the car floor. It is unwise to do so, even though they may double as a drain in the event of other accidental effluent, as it is likely to lead to corrosion!

Fortunately, many dogs are good

travellers and rarely appear very anxious, but remember that your anxiety can be communicated to the dog. Be nonchalant even if a pup is sick on most occasions and, instead, try to make it accept the car as a kind of playground. If that does not work, and you have run through all the old wives' tales put about by the so-called dog experts that abound in every neighbourhood, get advice from your vet.

Travel-training

Once a puppy has been persuaded to accept the car as an extension of the home (see page 40), you do not have much more to do. Gradually extending the journeys in the car on the way to those pleasurable experiences, such as a walk in the park, often conditions a puppy prone to motion sickness to being a good traveller.

This is not possible in every case, but it does tend to help those dogs whose own anxiety sets the nausea off. Of course, some owners will swear that mysterious 'fumes' or static electricity are the real cause. Those of the latter persuasion sometimes fit special earthing straps which trail from the bottom of the car along the road, perhaps choosing a matching colour to those furry dice in the back window. The idea is that the static electricity is thereby discharged and the journey will be less likely to be hampered by vomit. The fact that an earthing strap actually increases the risk of the car being struck by lightning is not usually stressed in the promotional literature of these items.

Preventing motion sickness

If all else fails and you are about to resign yourself to the fact that *your* dog is going to be sick every time you take it out in the car, you will have to go to your veterinary surgeon. It is possible to buy tablets on general sale that are intended to help control vomiting, but modern legislation in many countries rightly controls the most potent drugs as careless use by the layman can be harmful. Consequently those products on general sale are relatively innocuous and equally relatively ineffective.

Your friendly neighbourhood vet will willingly advise you on more efficacious methods. Tranquillizers are very effective in a high proportion of cases, especially in those where anxiety is the cause. However, if the anxiety is communicated to the dog by the owner, it is a pity the vet cannot prescribe a tranquillizer for the owner as well. That might be even more effective! The type of tablets most commonly prescribed for motion sickness are also useful for sedation (usually at a higher dose) before thunderstorms and for distress caused by fireworks.

It sometimes happens that following a few journeys under medication, the dog gains confidence and its vomit-inducing state of anxiety does not recur. However, tranquillizers can be somewhat unpredictable in their effect in that the lower dose levels used for controlling motion sickness may be too low for one dog and too high for another. This means that the pill either appears to have no effect at all or knocks the dog out for the count. In either case, contact your vet for advice on the change in dosage for *your* dog. If treatment is to condition your dog's behaviour in the car, either it must work or the dog must *know* it has worked. If the dog is fast asleep on the back seat (never encourage a dog to ride on the front seat) it will not recollect the journey nor benefit from the experience.

Leaving the dog in unattended cars

A dog is one of the best security systems for protecting a car, providing it is sufficiently aggressive to strangers who attempt to trespass on your property. That is another very good reason for training your puppy to look upon the car as an extension to the home.

If your dog is so soft that it licks trespassers to death, invest in one of the electronic warning and immobilizing devices (for the car, not the dog). However, do use a little intelligence when leaving your dog in the car. It is essential to ensure that ventilation is adequate, but, unless the winter is unusually typical of Siberia, there is no need to provide additional heat.

In summer, on the other hand, special care must be taken to avoid returning to the car to find that your pet is now a hot dog! Do not park the car in direct sunlight, and remember that the shade moves as the sun crosses the sky towards the west. If you are leaving the car for some time and shade is not provided by a substantial object such as a building, go back before the car is unprotected from direct sunlight so that it can be moved before it becomes an oven.

Ventilation is even more important in hot weather. One window needs to be opened far enough to allow a good circulation of air in the car, and probably more than one window, especially if the air is still. If your dog is an effective guard the car will be safe enough, but *do* ensure that the gap is not big enough to permit its head to go through, not to mention its body (see page 94). No passer-by relishes the prospect of an aggressive hound lunging out of a half-open window. If the weather is so hot that the window has to be open fairly wide, use one of the trellis-type window fillers that are available. These permit the window to be open without the dog getting out.

Leaving the dog

If you have to leave your dog while you go on holiday, there are a few alternatives to consider. It may be possible to have friends look after it for you in their own home, put the dog into a boarding kennels or have someone look after it in your own home.

Leaving the dog with friends

Providing your friends know and like the dog (and vice versa), this is probably the ideal arrangement. They should, however, know something about dogs in general and how to look after them, and have a dog-proof garden. No matter how obedient the dog is with you, it may well decide to play up with someone else – so ask them to keep it on a lead whenever they go out.

Leave them your vet's name, address and telephone number so that if there is any cause for concern they can take the dog to the practice that knows its history. In addition, it is advisable to write to the vet before you go, giving the name and address of the friend and authorizing the vet to treat the dog if it is brought in. You will also have to promise to pay on your return! Take the letter to your vet and ask him (do not assume) whether he will accept the arrangement. Although we all hope there is no necessity for it, this may save embarrassment should your dog run up a substantial bill during your absence. Consider the matter the other way round: if your plane makes an unscheduled landing on your return journey then your vet will be able to have his account paid by your executors!

Boarding the dog

Most owners have qualms about putting their dog into kennels, although this is not so disturbing if you have two dogs that get along well with each other and can be given a kennel to share. In fact, the majority of dogs seem to be quite content having *their* holiday, especially if there are very young children in the family! It is often said that if the owners knew how happy their dogs were in kennels, it would spoil their holiday!

Not that boarding the dog necessarily means a boarding kennels. There are private individuals (other than your friends) who take the occasional dog into their home for short periods (for a fee). Whether this appeals to you will depend on your opinion of the person and house

concerned. Whatever type of boarding establishment you go to, always inspect it before finalizing the booking. In the United Kingdom boarding kennels have to meet certain standards and be licensed by the local authority. This does not guarantee that a kennels will meet *your* ideals so it is always better to see for yourself. Any reluctance by the kennel management to permit inspection will confirm your worst fears and you will no doubt wish to look elsewhere.

It is no good trying to get your dog into kennels at the last minute if you are going away at the peak of the holiday season. The only vacancies are likely to be in the worst kennels. As soon as you know your holiday dates make your booking in the kennels of your choice.

Remember that the kennels will insist upon vaccination against some, if not all, of the common canine diseases. They should tell you their requirements when you make your booking, but remember to check the vaccination certificate from your vet to ensure that your dog is covered for those diseases up to the time of your return from holiday. The date when the next injection is due should be recorded on the certificate. If you are in *any* doubt, ask your vet. If a booster is required before going into kennels, ensure that it is given in good time and that the certificate is brought up to date.

If an establishment does not mention vaccination requirements, ask about them. They should demand to see the certificate when you take your dog in anyway, so remember to take it with you. Any kennels that do not undertake this kind of thorough inspection are likely to be slipshod, to say the least. You may make a mental note never to use them again, but in the meantime your dog will have to sample the dubious pleasure of their hospitality. That is why advance planning is so important.

Kennels usually feed a standard diet, but if there are medical reasons for your dog being on a special one they should be prepared to comply with its needs. However, these needs should be stated when booking the kennel accommodation and confirmed in writing. To make it doubly certain, take a copy of the diet when boarding the dog, and, if necessary, the diet itself.

If your dog is ill just prior to your going on holiday, ask your vet as to the wisdom of leaving it in kennels and whether it will put other residents at risk. And if the dog needs medication, you should obtain a letter from your vet outlining the treatment and certifying that there is no risk in accepting the dog for boarding. Armed with this, you should not encounter any problems in having your dog admitted.

Most kennels have their own favourite veterinary practice on whom they call

for treatment of their charges. This usually involves the vet visiting the kennels and obviously incurs a visit fee which you will have to meet. It may be that you would prefer to have your own vet see your pet. This should present no problem providing the kennels are within reach of your veterinarian and he is agreeable, but check with the kennels *before* you book and, again, confirm it in writing with them.

Leaving the dog at home

Leaving the dog in your own home is probably the most convenient way of coping with holidays where it cannot accompany you. The dog is in familiar surroundings, if missing you a little. Although one of the earliest animals to become domesticated by man, it has not yet become so domesticated that it cannot look after itself for a few days.

Whereas a cat can be fed once a day and allowed to go in and out at will through its cat-flap, things are not so simple for a dog. What you really need is a dog-sitter who doubles up as a home-sitter too, so reducing the risk of returning from holiday to an empty house with all the furniture gone. Again, like your friends, the dog-sitter should know and like your dog (and vice versa), know how to look after it and, perhaps, know how to look after your home.

Apart from the instructions for the dog, make sure that your volunteer knows where the vacuum cleaner is, how the dishwasher works and where to put the washing after he or she has ironed it. Leave the name and address of your destination as well as that of the vet, lock up the drinks cabinet if you are feeling particularly mean, and *bon voyage*.

Obviously, you should pick a home-cum-dog-sitter with great care. He or she should be well known to you, be completely trustworthy, dependable and prepared to do it for no more than the cost of boarding your dog, minus the cost of food for both. And, of course, there is all the housework to consider.

5. Fido's fitness

If your dog is to have a long and happy life you must take care to keep it fit and healthy. There are times when even the well-maintained car starts firing on only three cylinders or the batteries need charging. There will be times when the fittest dog is one degree under and needs slight adjustment, a service or even a major overhaul.

There is little point in having a dog, rearing it, training it and making it a member of your household unless you are going to keep it in good health and a credit to yourself. After all, if you neglect your dog to the point of it becoming a sickly, unkempt, smelly, flea-ridden travelling disaster area on four legs, who is going to blame the dog?

You owe it to your dog to keep it in first-class running order. Just as you notice that unusual noise in the car (even if you cannot always be too sure from

where it originates) and start to investigate it, so any unusual behaviour in your dog should elicit a similar response. Perhaps you do not know much about cars and decide to seek professional advice without more ado. That is very sound thinking, and you would be wise to adopt the same policy with your dog – providing you are not seeking advice from the local garage!

In fact there are only two things that it is important to know: first the signs of fitness or ill health in your dog and, second, a good vet to consult. If you have read Chapter 1, you should have found a vet already; and if not, get one organized now before it is too late.

Fitness or ill health?

If you are as observant with your dog as most parents are with their children, you will soon be able to notice those tell-tale signs that all is not well. Does your dog welcome you, as usual, in the morning when you come downstairs? Or does it stay in its bed? That is a sure sign that something is wrong. Has it lost interest in food? Does it drink excessively? Has it been unable to go through the night before without fouling the floor? Is it breathing faster than usual, without exertion? Are the eyes as bright and clear as usual or is there a discharge?

Does it have difficulty passing water or its motions? Or are the motions being passed with too much ease? Does it vomit?

However, ask most people what were the signs of a sick dog and they would reply a dry nose. Do not be misled by a dry nose. It is possible that the dog may have been sleeping curled up, with its nose under its hind leg, and the nose has dried out with the warmth.

Those are some of the common signs of illness, but there are many others, sometimes not easy to spot. There are a variety of signs involving the skin, for example. There may be loss of hair, or itching, which makes the dog scratch with its paws or teeth. Perhaps the dog is scratching or shaking its ears, rubbing its eyes, trying to nibble at its anal glands or rubbing its mouth on the ground because of a sore mouth or teeth. There are a hundred and one changes in behaviour that should be unmistakable signs to the observant owner that something is wrong. And remember that a dog does not have to be physically *ill* to be unfit. Once you appreciate that, you will soon find that you notice the warning signs at an early stage and so will be in a position to nip things in the bud.

There are a few helpful aids (not the disease – fortunately that is not a veterinary problem) which might be of value in some cases.

Taking the temperature

The first thing to remember is that you ought to have one thermometer for your pets and another for the family. In fact, it is not too dangerous to take the family thermometer and use it on the dog providing it is earmarked in future for pet use only and another bought for use by the family. Actually, earmarked is not the right word, as will very soon become clear.

The ideal glass thermometer should have a stub-ended bulb as this is less likely to break off inside the rectum than the long-bulbed variety. Even safer are the digital thermometers as these are virtually unbreakable, easy to read and do not have to be shaken vigorously like the traditional glass thermometer to get the mercury back into the bulb between one reading and the next. Indeed, the digital type does not need shaking at all. Its last reading is lost when it is switched off. Whether its cost is justified for one or two pets is another matter.

The technique for taking the temperature is simplicity itself, especially in the short-coated breeds, although it can sometimes be a problem to find the rectal orifice in the long-haired breeds, particularly in dim light.

The thermometer should be lubricated with liquid paraffin or Vaseline to facilitate insertion and, equally important, have someone hold the dog's head for you, as many dogs will resent what you are about to do. Ensure that the thermometer has been shaken down and reads below the dog's normal temperature. Holding the tail firmly in one hand (hard luck if you chose a close-docked breed), gently insert the thermometer about 1–2 in (2–5 cm) into the rectum. Keep hold of both tail and thermometer until the time is up (usually 30 seconds). Withdraw the thermometer and let go of the tail. If you let go of the tail first there is usually no need to withdraw the thermometer, often the dog will do it for you.

Having taken the temperature and read the thermometer, what does it all mean? The normal temperature of the dog is 101.5 °F (38.6 °C), with a range of 101–102.5 °F (38.3–39.1 °C). However, a normal temperature reading does not necessarily tell you very much if you have taken it only once. The animal may well have been ill and its temperature could have been higher but is now on the way down. And that is not always a good

sign. If the temperature carries on going down, death could be imminent. If it reaches room temperature, death has either taken place or there is a heat wave. In any event, a dog's temperature can be increased by strenuous exercise and even by hot weather. Therefore, you must not attach too much importance to the temperature but look at it in the light of any other signs that are present.

Checking respiratory rate

The respiratory rate is usually measured as the number of inspirations *and* expirations (the number of breaths) per minute. These will vary in the normal dog from one time to another, depending on a variety of factors.

Smaller dogs tend to breathe faster than larger dogs. The rate is increased by exercise, especially if it is vigorous and the dog is not used to it or is overweight. This is not altogether surprising. No doubt *you* would start panting rather earlier than an Olympic sprinter if you tried to keep up with one, providing you are not a gold medallist yourself, of course.

The respiratory rate is often increased

in pain, a stuffy atmosphere and, of course, when it is very hot. The dog does not cool itself down by perspiring, as we do, but by panting. In both cases the body is cooled by evaporation. In man it is an external, and in the dog an internal, cooling mechanism, and the difference lies in the fact that, unlike us, the dog has no sweat glands (except for a few between its toes) with which to cool off. In the resting dog the respirations may not be easily observed, especially in long-haired breeds. However, a look at chest and flank should give you a measure of inspiratory and expiratory movements.

It is a good idea to record the rate for *your* dog under normal conditions and compare the rate under stress, such as exercise or apprehensive states (perhaps car journeys, meeting strangers, trips to the vet), so that you have some idea of the norm for your pet. You will also be less likely to increase your own respiratory rate by worrying unnecessarily about the dog's, particularly if you make a needless visit to the vet and the sight of

the bill makes you take a sharp breath! The normal figure for the respiratory rate in the dog is 22 per minute, although this varies from one individual to another.

Taking the pulse

There are few occasions when an owner might usefully check a dog's pulse. Indeed, the only reason that could possibly be of any value is to determine whether the dog is alive or not. Obviously this is only likely in a dire emergency, such as a traffic accident, sudden heart failure or, possibly, poisoning.

There is a certain amount of expertise involved in interpretation of the pulse, so it is little value to you as a guide to Fido's fitness. However, the pulse is easily felt over the femoral artery, on the inside of the thigh (the back leg). If you are right-handed, have the dog in front of you, facing to your right. Insert the fingers inside the thigh, with the thumb outside the thigh. The artery should be felt throbbing under the fingers about midway along. It is just as well to know where it is. Have a feel for it from time to time and you will soon be versed in the art of finding it, even if you do not know what to do with it when you have done so.

The normal pulse rate in the dog is variable, in much the same way as the respiratory rate. It is usually between 80 and 100 per minute in a resting dog and increases on exercise, when agitated, or in pain and fear. If those states are removed then the pulse rate returns to normal. The pulse rate is also faster in the young dog, so if you establish the normal rate in a pup, this will slow down to some extent in the adult.

Anatomy of the dog

An elementary knowledge of the anatomy of the dog will be of value sometime in its life with you, even if only to help you understand what is going on when you have to take it to the vet. And there are occasions when it may help you to decide if you need to go to the vet at all.

The external parts of the dog are given in Figure 1. It is all straightforward, except to remind you that the forelegs are the equivalent of our arms. There is therefore an elbow and carpus (the wrist) instead of a knee and tarsus (the ankle) which are, of course, on the hind limbs.

The skeleton

There is considerable variation in the skeleton of the dog as regards the shape of the bones, depending on breed. For example, the shape of the skull of the Bulldog is very different from that of the

Figure 1. The external anatomy of the dog, showing the major parts.

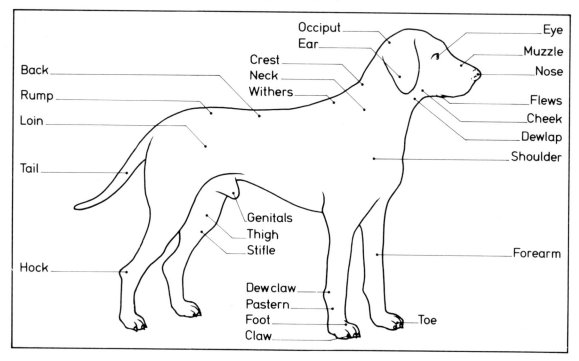

Greyhound, but then so are the legs. This makes a considerable difference to the way the two breeds behave and how fast they can run. Perhaps that is why nobody has ever initiated Bulldog racing! Nor used Greyhounds in fighting bulls.

Apart from the obvious differences in the size of animal influencing the size of the bones, there are also differences in shape. The short-legged dogs are ideal examples. The limbs of some are basically smaller versions of the longer-legged varieties. The Toy and Miniature Poodles are similar in proportion to the Standard Poodle. Other breeds, such as the Dachshund and Basset Hound, are a little grotesque, having bowed front legs.

The number of vertebrae is standard in all dogs from head-to-nearly-the-tail. There are 20–23 coccygeal vertebrae (the bones that constitute the tail), or at least there are at birth. Unfortunately, the barbaric advocates of tail docking often reduce them to a handful in order to 'improve' on nature, which means purely for the purposes of fashion. The few that are left can scarcely be said to wag happily along behind.

Other appendages often removed shortly after birth are the dew claws, or rudimentary toes. These are useless evolutionary hangovers on the legs of some, but not all, dogs – rather like the human appendix. However, they can be a disadvantage to some dogs, being liable to get caught and torn or to grow round and into the adjacent pad, and so are best taken off unless they are regarded as a desirable feature for show purposes, as is the case with the Pyrennean Mountain Dog, for example, which has double dew claws on each hind leg.

The internal organs

The internal organs and their respective roles are most easily understood as separate systems with their constituent parts.

The body, by which we mean the whole animal less its head and limbs, is divided into two, but not necessarily equal, halves by the diaphragm. The anterior 'half' is the thorax and the posterior 'half' the abdomen. The illustration shows the sites of the major internal organs.

The respiratory system and the heart are housed in the thorax. The greater part of the digestive and urogenital systems are in the abdomen. The nervous and circulatory systems consist of networks everywhere in the animal. Each system will be considered in turn over the next few pages.

The respiratory system

The respiratory system comprises the nasal passages, the mouth and pharynx (these two being shared with the digestive system), and the larynx (bark box), which leads into the trachea (windpipe) which divides into two bronchi (left and right). Both bronchi divide into two again prior to entering the two lungs (right and left). Do not be confused, the left bronchi do go to the left lung and the right bronchi to the right lung.

ATCHOO!!

To be strictly accurate, even pedantic, the bronchi may not always go to the lungs. Sometimes they come *from* the lungs. It all depends on whether the dog is breathing in or out at the time.

Barking, coughing and sneezing need more than simple relaxation of the inspiratory muscles in the dog's chest. Here, the animal uses abdominal muscles and others in the ribs. In some conditions, where the blood is unable to obtain enough oxygen by normal respiratory movements, this abdominal respiration is used to try to obtain more oxygen. Some owners take this as a sign of respiratory disease. It may well be, but it might also be due to blood circulatory problems.

The circulatory system

To all intents and purposes this system may be compared to a central heating system. It consists of a pump (the heart), feed pipes (the arteries), the radiators (the organs) and the return pipes (the veins).

A central heating system is intended simply to provide heat in various parts of the house and water carries the heat from the boiler to the radiators, but in fact the body's circulatory system has more than one function. It not only provides warmth when it is required but also carries round the raw materials for the various body activities: oxygen, fats, carbohydrate, protein, vitamins and minerals. These are not picked up in any one place. There are, in fact, several 'boilers' in the circulatory system. Oxygen, as mentioned earlier, is picked up in the lungs and the nutritional compounds from the intestinal circulation. Some of those substances are stored in various parts of the body, such as the liver, and fat is deposited about the place as some of us are far too well aware.

The blood also serves a very important function in defence against illness. Apart from the red blood cells – they are actually green when viewed individually under the microscope, but whoever heard of green blood cells? – there are also white blood cells. These cells are the frontline troops in the fight against germs in the body and also clear away cell debris, bacteria and small foreign bodies. It is these cells that are to be found in pus and give it its white or creamy appearance.

Red blood cells contain a substance called haemoglobin which combines with oxygen at the lungs for transport around the body to the tissues, where it sheds the oxygen and combines with carbon dioxide for transport back to the lungs. It is obvious that haemoglobin plays a vital part in body function. A deficiency of haemoglobin can have very serious effects. As iron is an element in the molecule, an iron deficiency results in anaemia. Vitamin B12 is essential for haemoglobin production and a deficiency results in pernicious anaemia.

Arteries carry the oxygenated blood *from* the heart to all parts of the body and are thick-walled. Being directly connected to the heart, they reflect the heartbeats in the pulse. When cut, the bright red arterial blood spurts out in a typical manner.

Veins, on the other hand, are thin-walled and carry carbon-dioxide-laden blood back *to* the heart. When these are cut the blood runs out without the spurt observed with severed arteries. This piece of general knowledge is of value in knowing where to apply a tourniquet in the event of accidents – see page 110 for more details.

The nervous system

The nervous system comprises the brain and the nerves that connect it with the various parts of the body. The nerves not only go from the brain to those parts; there are also nerves from those parts to the brain.

In other words, just as arteries carry blood from the heart to all parts of the body and veins to carry it back to the heart, so there are nerves carrying messages *from* the brain and others that carry messages back *to* the brain. Some of those messages from the brain are as a result of conscious effort, but others, such as circulation of the blood, are quite automatic. There are also reflexes which do not involve messages going to the brain at all. We are all familiar with the knee-jerk reflex, in which a slight blow below the knee results in the automatic forward movement of the foot. Dogs are equipped with a similar system.

The digestive system

You will recollect that the mouth and throat are shared with the respiratory system. The food is taken into the mouth and often, but not always, chewed. In the process it is mixed with saliva which contains enzymes to initiate the digestive processes, which break down food into simpler substances. The dog's digestive system copes well with unmasticated food, so do not worry unduly if your dog does not chew its food but bolts it down as if there were no tomorrow. However, if a dog habitually gulps its food, it is better to feed minced meat rather than large pieces.

At the back of the throat the food and water go down the oesophagus, a long pipe which passes through the middle of the chest cavity and diaphragm into the stomach. Here they are churned around

with the gastric juices to further the digestive process. Food remains in the stomach for a variable period before passing into the small intestine. Generally, the contents of the stomach will have passed into the intestines by four hours after a meal but can take longer on some occasions. Food is only partially digested in the stomach – the intestines take care of the real job of breaking it down into compounds the body can use.

As the food passes down the intestines mixed with the digestive juices, it has become more liquid. Its passage down the gut is relatively slow and in the large intestine (at the tail end) the water is absorbed through the gut wall. As the inexorable progress of the bowel contents continues towards the light at the end of the tunnel, they become drier and are packed into the rectum in the form familiar to us all.

The liver

The liver is the largest organ in the body and although it contributes to the digestive processes in supplying bile, it has much more important functions that are vital to health. For example, the protein, fat and carbohydrates that are absorbed from the intestines into the blood pass through the liver, where they are changed into substances for storage for the future or into those the body can utilize.

Further, the liver is a vital organ in that it converts many poisonous substances into compounds that are less poisonous. It stores certain vitamins and iron; it is involved in the production of red blood cells, plasma and fibrinogen (which is the blood clotting protein).

The urogenital system

Urine contains more of the waste products of the body. It is produced in the kidneys (of which there are two). The kidneys are, in effect, filters. Interference in kidney function through disease, therefore, can either prevent adequate excretion of waste products and lead to their accumulation in the bloodstream or result in the loss of substances that an efficient kidney normally retains.

Either way, kidney disease can spell

trouble. There is a tendency to think that when a dog is passing more water with greater frequency this is because its fluid intake has increased recently. There is a certain logic in that thought, based on personal experience at the bar, no doubt. In fact, although it can be true, it is really a case of putting the cart before the horse. If the urine output has increased because the kidneys are less efficient, the body loses more water than usual and the relative dehydration that follows creates thirst. So the dog drinks more.

There is also the matter of how urine passes from the kidneys to the outside. Each kidney is connected to the bladder by a tube called a ureter. Urine is produced by the kidneys continuously and it passes down each ureter to the bladder where it is stored. From here, it proceeds to the outside world via the urethra, in both dog and bitch. As in man, the emptying of the bladder can be controlled consciously – although judging by some dogs you would be forgiven for thinking that they had no consciousness of the fact at all.

The urethra empties through the floor of the vagina close to the vulva in the bitch or passes to the outside through the penis in the dog. The penis of the dog has a 'bone' in it, called the *os penis*, which is not actually made of bone but of cartilage.

The *os penis* is V-shaped in cross-section, in the same shape as an angle iron (Ouch!, some human males may say). The urethra passes through the penis in the 'V' which can present a problem in dogs with urinary calculi (stones formed in the urine by deposits of salts). In the bitch there is usually no problem when these are passed down the urethra, apart from some discomfort. However, a problem can develop in the dog if the diameter of the stones is greater than the width of the *os penis*. This results in a blockage and inability to pass urine. Fortunately, such problems can be overcome by surgery, although the treatment may dramatically affect the dog's sexual effectiveness. Your dog may reflect that this is infintely preferable to an exploding bladder; your veterinarian certainly will.

The genital part of the urogenital system will be discussed in its proper place – in Chapter 8 (see pages 112–19).

Hormones

There are a number of ductless glands in the body that produce substances called hormones which play very important roles in the way it performs.

The ductless glands produce only very small amounts of hormones, but their effects are profound. Some hormones exert their influence rapidly and others act more slowly. Some glands produce several hormones, each with specific effects, and a hormone from one gland may influence the output of another. The important point to remember is that in a healthy animal one hormone is often in balance with one or more others and disturbance of the overall hormonal balance may have harmful effects. The main glands that might be mentioned by your vet include the adrenals, pituitary, thyroid, parathyroid, ovary, testicle and pancreas.

Localized conditions

There are a number of conditions in the dog affecting certain parts of the body that are not always caused by specific infections; indeed, often not. These are reviewed in the remainder of this chapter.

Anal gland problems

The anal glands are the two scent glands situated one on each side of the rectum. The duct from each gland opens on either side of the anus. If you imagine the anus as a somewhat revolting clockface, the openings are to be seen at four and eight o'clock, if you look carefully. Actually, they are still there if you do not look at all. If the duct becomes blocked, the continued secretion results in enlarged, overfull glands which cause irritation at the tail end.

Normally the passing of faeces gently squeezes the glands and a small amount of secretion is extruded. A bout of diarrhoea, or even a tendency to produce motions with a softer consistency, can mean that the gland is not properly squeezed and therefore contains as much secretion after a motion is passed as it did before. If this goes on for some days, the secretion may dry up and block the duct. In other cases, the glands may become infected, possibly so badly that an abscess is formed. If untreated, the abscess may rupture and discharge the contents through the skin instead of through the duct. Anal glands that give intense irritation and pain when motions are passed may well cause the dog to become constipated. Indeed, this is a frequent sequel to abscessed glands.

Such problems are easy to spot. The dog will make clear by its behaviour that something is worrying it at the back end. It may 'scoot' its rear along the floor or try to nibble at it. Neither approach provides relief; indeed, sores may result, depending on the texture of the floor surface.

If your dog is nibbling the skin in one or two areas at the back end (near the root of the tail, between the hind legs, even just in front of the hind legs if the dog is incapable of reaching any further back) and/or 'scooting', suspect a problem with anal glands and take it to the vet. Increasing the fibre content of the diet, for example with bran, can help those dogs particularly prone to anal gland problems.

Arthritis

Arthritis means inflammation of a joint (dope fiends may find this confusing, but that is another matter). As in man, arthritis can affect animals of any age and is not confined to the old, even though it is more common in the elderly.

The joint may become inflamed following injury, including direct blows, dislocations, strain of the joint capsule and ligaments or, in some cases, from congenital instability. Inflammation leads to enlargement of the joint, increase in joint fluid and even pus where infection has been introduced into the joint.

In septic arthritis the joint is not only enlarged, it is hot and painful. The body temperature may well be up and the dog is usually very lame. It is possible that you will be able to see the wound through which infection was introduced into the joint. This is usually obvious in bite wounds, or knowledge of a recent fight may lead you to suspect a cause-and-effect relationship.

It is wise to take your dog to your vet if it is bitten by another dog anyway, but doubly so if it is bitten very near a joint as septic arthritis is better prevented than cured. This is because the all-important smooth cartilage can be partially destroyed by the pus and result in a permanently lame dog, even if the infection is cleared up.

Osteoarthritis – where both bone and joint are inflamed – is commonly associated with advancing age. The affected joints may well have been injured earlier in life and obesity increases the strain on them – in old age there is a tendency to exercise less and put on weight. Therefore, any tendency to obesity should be controlled if there is a significant history of lameness.

Fortunately, rheumatoid arthritis does not occur in dogs but osteoarthritis can be equally difficult to control. There are treatments that can help to slow up the progressive nature of the condition and it can be possible to provide some relief from pain.

Hip dysplasia

Hip dysplasia is an abnormality in the hip joint that occurs mainly in larger and medium-sized breeds such as the Labrador, German Shepherd or Rottweiler. Although it is congenital (that is, the dog is born with it) and heredity plays a major part, there is no doubt that environmental factors influence whether a dog becomes lame or not, and to what extent.

The hip is a 'ball-and-socket' joint, the 'socket' being on the pelvis and the 'ball' at the head of the femur or thigh bone. The normal hip joint is a snug fit without any play. In hip dysplasia the 'ball' is not completely engaged by the 'socket' because the head of the femur is flattened to some degree and the 'socket' is too shallow.

The degree of abnormality can vary from one individual to another. Not all dogs with hip dysplasia will show signs of lameness; it depends on the degree of abnormality and the way the dog is reared and kept. An affected dog which habitually jumps down from a height may well develop symptoms, whereas a less active dog with worse hip dysplasia might get through its life without showing any lameness at all.

Symptoms include difficulty lying down and getting up, an obviously abnormal swaying of the rear end when walking, avoiding the use of the hind legs where possible and discomfort, if not pain, when rising, walking, running or even standing.

Since there are hereditary aspects of hip dysplasia the best approach is not to breed from affected animals. In the United Kingdom, breeders of dysplasia-prone animals are co-operating in a screening programme to assess whether breeding stock are free of the abnormality. In this way the incidence can be reduced, providing the public buys puppies bred only from certified dogs and bitches. Your vet will be able to supply you with more details.

Nephritis

Nephritis is inflammation of the kidney. There are a number of causes of kidney diseases but these come more within the province of the vet than the owner. Acute interstitial nephritis occurs less commonly nowadays, largely due to the high proportion of dogs being vaccinated against leptospirosis (see Chapter 6,

page 91) in the past 25 years. Far more common is glomerulonephritis (GN) which is often followed by progressive kidney failure. If there is loss of appetite, wasting of muscles and massive protein loss in the urine, a special diet is almost certainly needed.

Chronic kidney failure is the sequel to such kidney diseases, in which a large amount of functional tissue is lost over a continuing period. There is a marked thirst and an increase in urine output in the early stages, with occasional vomiting. Although there may be other, less serious reasons for an increase in water intake and urination, symptoms of this kind should lead you and your dog to the vet without delay.

Cystitis

Cystitis is inflammation of the bladder and is often accompanied by inflammation of the urethra, or urethritis. Unless you knew beforehand, you will

now have realized that the suffix '-itis' means 'inflammation of'.

The observant owner keeps an eye on a pet's natural physiological functions because passing water and faeces are two important clues to a dog's well-being. They are as useful indicators as its intake of food and water. Indeed, the passing of motions does depend to some extent upon the eating of food!

A dog with cystitis passes water more frequently, or at least tries to do so – the flow might not be as free as usual. There may be some blood in the urine, especially at the end of the process. More frequent urination is easier to observe in the bitch, which does not have the male dog's propensity for watering every lamp-post or tree in its path (or even off its path). Most male dogs have owners who have long since given up trying to distinguish between waterworks problems and the urge to scent-mark everything in sight.

Pharyngitis

Pharyngitis, inflammation of the pharynx, is a sore throat. When the throat is sore it hurts to swallow, so when your dog tries to eat and stops, or swallows with some difficulty, the chances are that it is not seriously ill but just has a sore throat. However, that is no reason to sit back and ignore your pet's discomfort on the grounds that a ticklish throat never did anyone much harm. First, it might be the first sign of a more serious condition, secondly something else might flare up and thirdly your dog may not get better on its own for days.

Vomiting

Vomiting can occur for several reasons – eating something irritant to the stomach, for example, or even sheer greed. It could be a chemical irritant, rotten food (possibly contaminated with bacteria, or merely irritant in its decomposed form), bone splinters, or just ordinary food if the stomach is inflamed and thus more sensitive to what gets put into it.

If the dog vomits once and seems to be as bright as usual afterwards, there is probably no cause for concern, except over mopping-up operations. Even if it seems one degree under, you need not worry unduly providing the problem does not persist for more than an hour or two. Bear in mind also that when a dog feels under the weather it will often eat grass, given the chance. This is invariably followed by vomiting the grass and the rest of the stomach contents, probably a clear or frothy mucus.

So far there is little to worry about. That comes when the dog vomits at frequent intervals and is obviously ill. The main question is why: might there be a stoppage in the bowel, for example? If you have not seen whether the dog is passing faeces, ask the family in case they have noticed. Any undue delay in its natural functions could well suggest a blockage. On the other hand, perhaps there is diarrhoea as well as vomiting. Has anyone given the dog any bones or unusual food? Collect all available evidence and go down to the vet for treatment as soon as possible.

Vomiting may be a symptom of the toxic dog, not only a sign of trouble in the digestive system. It should be looked upon as a serious problem if it persists.

Diarrhoea

Diarrhoea, like vomiting, can follow ingestion of an irritant. Diarrhoea is a frequent sequel to a hot curry, for example, and not only in man. Dogs belonging to those from the Indian subcontinent can develop the taste, and possibly the diarrhoea, with ease!

Whenever you see your dog has diarrhoea at two consecutive motions it is wise to take the dog of meat. As the food is passing down the intestines too fast for complete digestion of the meat, it only encourages the diarrhoea. Give lightly boiled or scrambled egg with boiled rice, which is easily digested.

Growths

The use of the euphemism 'growth' rather than 'cancer' is intentional. People tend to have a phobia about cancer, in themselves or their pets, based on the assumption that you can do little to cure or prevent it.

However, medical knowledge has vastly improved over the years and although there are limits to what can be done, it is always better to do it today rather than tomorrow. There is more chance of successful surgery in the early stages and less chance that a cancer may have already spread to other parts of the body. Having said that, bear in mind that not all tumours are cancers. A cancer is a malignant growth that usually, but not always, occurs in the older animal. When it starts to grow it generally does so at a faster rate than the harmless, benign tumour.

If you notice a small lump somewhere on or in the dog's body, make a mental note of its size, unless you decide to sprint to the vet at the next available surgery, and keep an eye on it. Do not check progress daily or you will be unable to tell whether it is growing. Check it weekly.

The commonest suspected tumours are generally benign or not tumours at all, for example fatty lumps (lipomas) under the skin, which are absolutely harmless. Lumps on the skin are usually warty lesions or papillomas, or they may be sebaceous cysts. The surgical removal of lipomas is for cosmetic rather than health reasons. The warty lesions and sebaceous cysts are frequently left alone unless they are disfiguring (usually in the short-coated breeds), a focus for nibbling or liable to get caught and bleed.

There *are* occasions when the vet has to break the news to you that there *is* a cancer or a risk of one developing. Be advised by your vet who knows rather more about the relative risks than you do, but do not automatically assume the worst. Surgery is not so terrible as you may be inclined to think and often it can be completely successful. This is one situation where it is so true that a stitch in time saves nine! Once a growth has been removed, it is usually sent to a laboratory for pathological examination to confirm whether it was benign or malignant. It is *sometimes* possible to be certain that it is one or the other on physical appearance alone, but not very often. The important thing, in any case of this kind, is to seek advice as soon as possible.

Mammary growths

Tumours of the mammary glands deserve a special mention as they are sufficiently common to keep an eye open for. They are usually detected quite early as the bitch enjoys being stroked along the mammary glands and owners frequently do so. Although benign tumours of the mammary gland do occur, there is a risk of their becoming malignant. It is sensible to have them removed as soon as they are detected.

There is evidence that some of these growths are 'hormone dependent', but a specialized laboratory test is needed to determine whether this is so. Until the laboratory service is made more widely available the only treatment is surgery.

Pyometra

Pyometra is a condition in bitches in which the womb fills with pus. It is not due to infection but is the result of hormonal disturbance. Although younger animals can suffer from it, the problem is most common in those over five years old. Typically, the bitch will have finished its last heat in the previous eight weeks, the abdomen will begin to swell and the responsible owner will suspect an Immaculate Conception (as the responsible owner will know that it could not be anything else).

Pyometra occurs most commonly in bitches that have bred irregularly or not at all. There is a popular misconception – if that is the right word – that allowing a bitch to have one litter will prevent the development of the condition. This is quite untrue.

There are two forms, termed open and closed pyometra. In the closed case the cervix remains shut tight and the pus collects in the uterus, hence the tubby abdomen. All cases start off closed. If the cervix dilates and lets the pus drain to the outside, it is termed an open pyometra. Most owners are not exactly happy about that situation, as if they had wanted mottled carpets they would have bought them in the first place. However, from the bitch's point of view it is better to have open pyometra than closed, as the potentially toxic uterine contents are not being bottled up and making the animal feel *really* ill.

There is likely to be loss of appetite in both forms, but the closed case will grow ill quite rapidly, becoming depressed, showing excessive thirst and vomiting. She will pass water more frequently and unless something is done will certainly die, but not of old age.

Until recently, surgery was the only life-saving option, involving the complete removal of ovaries and uterus. New treatments with prostaglandins have been used with success in some cases, although as yet no pharmaceutical company will actually recommend them for this purpose.

Dermatitis

Inflammation of the skin can be caused by fungi (ringworm), bacteria, external parasites (mange, ticks and fleas) and of course any trauma such as wounds, scalds, chemical irritants and allergies. Whatever the primary cause it usually pales into insignificance compared to the effects of the self-inflicted trauma caused by the dog itself. One of the commonest sites of dermatitis is the area around the tail which was referred to when discussing anal gland problems (see page 80).

Half the battle in dermatitis is the control of pruritus (itching). The dog has an itch so it scratches; the more it scratches the more it itches; the more it itches the more it scratches. This is called the itch–scratch cycle. So, apart from the primary cause, there is a secondary cause that has to be controlled first.

Stop the itch and there is every hope that you can control the primary cause. Physical prevention of scratching (with claws or teeth) or licking the affected parts is neither easy nor helpful to the dog. Pruritus becomes more intense at night when all is quiet, just as the dripping tap on the bedroom wash-basin gets louder as you drop off to sleep.

Dental problems

Once your dog is about four or five years old, keep an eye on its teeth. A filthy mouth is the first step to ill health and bad breath, and it is far better to prevent trouble than to try to patch it up when things are too far gone. Ask your vet to carry out a quick dental check-up when you take your dog in for its annual vaccination booster.

If tartar is allowed to build up on the teeth, the gums recede and infection is likely to be introduced into the teeth sockets and the teeth themselves become loose. It allows food to accumulate and ferment, encouraging gingivitis (inflammation of the gums). All that wipes the smile off your dog's face and the cost of treatment will do the same to you.

6. Canine ailments

Specific diseases

There are several infections that cause specific disease in dogs. The following pages will deal with some of the more important of them.

From the previous chapter you will already know how to tell if your dog is ill, but unless you are a veterinarian you will be unlikely to know exactly what is wrong with it. Particular symptoms of one disease may be shared by other conditions and the important thing is to know when to take your dog to the vet for expert diagnosis. As with any condition, the key to successful treatment is to catch it early and hit it hard.

Canine parvovirus

Canine parvovirus infection is a recent disease that suddenly appeared in the late 1970s. The first case was recorded in 1977 in Texas and the causal virus isolated. The first cases in the British Isles occurred a year later and there were soon reports confirming its existence in every country in which pet dogs were plentiful.

A parvovirus infection of cats has been in existence for many years, being the virus that causes feline enteritis. So long as the virus attacked only cats there was little to worry about – of course, there was a lot to worry about if you were a cat – but then by what is termed a mutation the virus was able to change its structure and attack other animals. It first attacked American mink and then changed again and went for raccoons. The parvovirus that affects dogs appears to be yet another mutation, and before long vets were having to tackle an unexpected and deadly foe.

An adult dog has more resistance to the virus than a young puppy, so the effects of a hitherto unknown disease in the adult population did not immediately attract much attention. The symptoms in the adult are those of gastro-enteritis, namely vomiting and diarrhoea, and similar symptoms had been seen in dogs for many, many years. To vets, it simply appeared a case of too many upset tummies. And although an adult dog *can* die of parvovirus, mortality in dogs over the age of six months was of the order of an insignificant 1 per cent, hardly a cause for much concern.

The potential severity of the disease only really became clear when it was introduced into dog breeding establishments. A characteristic of the virus is that it establishes itself in cells that are actively dividing. The most rapidly dividing cells in puppies up to the age of three weeks are those of the heart. The virus therefore causes heart disease

when a pup picks up infection in that age range.

When parvo (as it has come to be known) hit the breeding kennels, where there are often several litters up to eight or nine weeks of age, there was severe illness in very young puppies and a 70–80 per cent mortality rate. Puppies of five weeks upwards showed the typical symptoms of acute gastro-enteritis and a death rate of 10 per cent.

It is interesting to note that around three to four weeks of age the pups are being weaned, as a result of which the most actively dividing cells are in the gut. This explains why, in slightly older puppies, the parvovirus goes for the gut instead of the heart.

Protection against parvovirus

Eventually – and not before time – manufacturers were able to develop effective vaccines. There is, however, a catch.

The newborn puppy is extremely susceptible to parvovirus infection and, besides, it is hardly practical to vaccinate such a tiny creature. In any case, immunity to any disease takes time to develop. Protection is best afforded by ensuring that the mother's own immunity is well developed before whelping, for in this way the bitch passes on a temporary immunity, which will last for several weeks, to the puppy in its milk over the first day or two of life.

However, this variable persistence of passive immunity, as it is known, presents problems in planning a parvovirus vaccination programme for puppies because the maternally derived antibodies (MDA) can interfere with the vaccine given to the puppy. Some puppies have low levels of MDA because the bitch did not have a high level herself. Others, born to a bitch with high antibody levels, have a high level of MDA.

Puppies with a high level at, say, eight

or nine weeks may not respond to their first dose of vaccine, although as they are already protected via their mother this does not matter. On the other hand, if a puppy has a low level of MDA then the vaccine at eight or nine weeks may well elicit a response and the pup will start to produce its own antibodies. The first dose of vaccine is therefore rather like an insurance policy. We all take out fire insurance in case the house catches fire, but we do not complain if it does not do so!

The problem comes when the second dose is to be given at about 12 weeks old. Apparently there are some puppies that have such high levels of MDA (as judged by a certain blood test) that they are alleged to produce inadequate immunity. As a result, some experts have made dogmatic statements to the effect that puppies should be vaccinated against parvo at 8, 12 and 20 weeks or even a super luxury job of 8, 12, 16 and 20 weeks! And the puppy must be kept from contact with other dogs for two weeks after the last dose. Your vet will know the circumstances in your area and will advise you on the best course of treatment to protect your dog.

Picking up parvovirus

Other reasons why canine parvovirus is such a serious disease are its resistance to many common disinfectants, its ability to survive independently where dogs have shed the virus and its ability to be carried on clothes and footwear. The virus would appear to be virtually everywhere in the environment where dogs go. It is therefore essential to maintain your

dog's immunity by keeping up with booster vaccinations in accordance with your vet's recommendations.

Infectious canine hepatitis

This is largely a problem of the past, at least in those areas where a high proportion of the dog population is vaccinated against the common canine diseases.

It is caused by yet another virus and can affect dogs of any age. Infection is usually gained by mouth. The virus can be carried on clothes and shoes, but it is also spread by direct contact between dogs as the virus is present in all of the secretions and excretions during the acute stages of the illness. The virus finally settles in the kidney and can be excreted for several months in the urine after recovery. There is an increase in temperature for several days, marked lethargy, loss of appetite, runny eyes and nose, thirst, tonsillitis and possibly vomiting. In the more severely affected cases there can be interference with blood clotting which is shown by bleeding in the mouth and haematomas (blood blisters).

The disease can easily be fatal, and although those that recover will start to eat again they will take a long time to put on the weight they have lost. One in four dogs that recover show a transient corneal opacity – called 'blue eye' – which disappears without treatment.

Canine distemper

Distemper, or 'hard pad' as it is sometimes called, is a highly contagious viral disease and had been a problem for many, many years until the advent of a vaccine in the 1930s, although this had side-effects. Today, more effective vaccines have made such problems a thing of the past and puppies are treated quite safely and given a booster at regular intervals. As a result, the incidence of distemper is far lower than it used to be and most cases are in dogs that have not been vaccinated at all or that have not been given booster injections.

The classic symptoms of the disease are an increase in temperature for a day or so followed by an apparent return to normal until it rises again several days later. The first fever is often missed or ignored by the owner, who simply thinks that the dog is having an off day. The second fever is much more obvious and the dog is clearly very ill. The eyes are full of mucus and pus, there is a nasal discharge, conjunctivitis, lethargy and loss of appetite, diarrhoea and, often, pneumonia.

You don't often see a dog with distemper these days.

The visible signs of the first, feverish stage are mainly due to bacterial infections which are secondary to the viral infection itself. These generally respond to antibiotic treatment but antibiotics are not active against a virus. The distemper virus damages brain cells and in a high proportion of cases the full effects of the damage, ranging from minor nervous complications to severe convulsions, do not appear until recovery from the first stage is well underway. There is little that can be done in such cases; it entirely depends on the severity of the brain damage, although anticonvulsants can help to minimize the nervous symptoms.

A few dogs have been nursed back to health after a bout of distemper but the odds are extremely thin and the care required is very demanding. Euthanasia is really the only option if nervous symptoms start to appear.

Leptospirosis

There are two forms of leptospirosis in dogs. One affects the kidneys (known colloquially as lamp-post disease) and the other the liver. The second also infects other mammals, including man (in whom it is known as Weil's disease). Modern vaccines give protection against both kinds.

'Lamp-post disease' was very common until vaccines were developed, and although the problem was fairly easy to cure many victims were left with chronic nephritis – which is what you would expect from a kidney infection. An infection of the liver, on the other hand, is much more serious. It leads to jaundice and is frequently fatal. This kind is generally picked up through contact with infected urine and rats are usually the reservoir of infection. If a dog shows signs of jaundice, namely yellow discoloration of the skin and mucous membranes, avoid contact with the urine in case this infection is present.

Immunity to leptospirosis does not persist for as long as some of the other diseases that can be vaccinated against. Whereas you *can* get away with boosting the immunity against those a little late, it is wisest to keep your appointment for a jab against this infection.

Kennel cough

This is the last of the diseases against which dogs are commonly vaccinated and is fortunately a mild one. Technically, it is an infectious tracheobronchitis characterized by a dry, spasmodic, harsh cough which is frequently stimulated by excitement. It is caused by a virus combined with a bacterial infection, called *Bordetella bronchiseptica*.

There is some difference of opinion as to which infection is most important, but since both play a part perhaps it is academic. Both are spread by droplet infection via the atmosphere – like the common cold in man – which means that cold, draughty and enclosed conditions provide the ideal breeding ground for the disease. Most cases used to occur in dogs that had been in kennels during the owner's absence on holiday, hence the name, but more recently there has been an increased incidence of the disease in dogs that have no recent history of a sojourn in kennels.

An infected dog will show no loss of appetite and may be untroubled while at rest but prone to a bout of coughing whenever it is excited. Usually these occasions are obvious, such as when you come down in the morning, pick up the lead to go for a walk or a visitor arrives. In mild cases the cough is unproductive, but in severe ones varying amounts of mucus are brought up which, if not swallowed, may be confused with vomit. There may even be gagging and retching.

The problem here is inflammation of the windpipe and bronchi. The mucous glands lining the airways are producing more mucus than usual and in addition there is likely to be ulceration of the lining itself. The lining has miriads of tiny hairs on it that carry the mucus to the back of the throat, but the loss of hairs in the ulcerated areas causes the mucus to accumulate and then fall back down to the bottom of the airway. The only way to clear it is to cough it up. The severity of the cough therefore reflects the amount of mucus and the extent of surface damage.

Appropriate antibacterial treatment to control the inflammation and reduce the output of mucus will usually reduce the frequency of coughing and its duration. However, the restoration of the hairs in the lining of the bronchi has to await the body's own repair system. Some cases, fortunately a minority, suffer such extensive damage that they will have a cough for the rest of their lives, but a reasonable proportion of dogs are back to normal in two to three weeks.

The vaccines used to prevent kennel cough have had variable results so far. In any case, the incidence of the disease varies widely from one area to another and vaccination may be an unnecessary precaution. Ask your vet about the value of vaccination in your area.

Rabies

Only a few countries (including Britain) are free of rabies. It was eliminated in Britain in 1902, although an outbreak occurred in 1918 probably as a result of a dog being smuggled in by a soldier returning from continental Europe. The importation of susceptible animals into the United Kingdom requires both an import licence and obligatory quarantine for six months, at considerable cost. If irresponsible smugglers were putting only their own lives at risk their selfish motives might be acceptable, but rabies is both highly contagious and deadly,

and the danger of it spreading cannot be over-emphasized.

Rabies is a virus transmitted by bites. Although the virus is present in the saliva of infected animals it has its effects on the nervous system. There is a long incubation period, usually up to six months in the dog, and the saliva is infective for several days before symptoms actually appear. The first one is a change in behaviour, often aggression. You should always suspect the possibility of rabies if bitten by an animal in any country where the disease is endemic, particularly if the aggression is out of character for the animal or if you are unable to find out whether it is or not. Get medical advice as soon as possible.

Although rabies vaccines for dogs are available, vaccination against the disease is not permitted in Britain lest it make cases more difficult to identify should an outbreak occur.

Timing vaccinations

We have now established that dogs are commonly vaccinated against distemper, infectious hepatitis, leptospirosis and canine parvovirus. It is also possible to vaccinate against kennel cough but this is something of an optional extra.

Opposite: *Some dogs always insist on second helpings – like some owners. Do not give in: happy hounds are healthy, not overweight.*

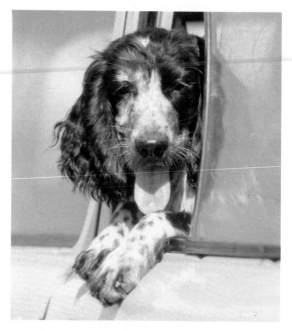

Left: *The car-bound hound needs plenty of air, but not so much that passers-by can be flagged down by a questing paw.*

Below: *Friend or foe? Young pups get all the exercise they need from play, but do make that garden dog-proof!*

Opposite above: *Some dogs adore water, but you should never encourage one to cool off in the swimming pool.*

Opposite below: *An energetic dog needs an energetic owner – otherwise you, rather than the dog, will be seeking treatment first.*

The companies that make vaccines have their own recommendations for their products, but unfortunately not all conform with one another. There is often an age range for first doses and each veterinary practice will make its own decision as to the ideal timing, in the light of its own local knowledge.

Table 5 gives a basic scheme of timing for first and second doses with the additional suggestions on the extra doses of parvovirus vaccine mentioned earlier on page 89. Broadly speaking, vaccination can start at six weeks of age with the second dose at 12 weeks of age or over (but not earlier). If the first dose is given as late as over ten weeks old, the second dose *must* be given *at least* 14 days after the first.

Two further points. Do not think that vaccines automatically confer immunity from disease, as surely as night follows day. It is not as simple as that. It depends on the strength of the vaccine, on the level of the challenge to it and on the ability of the individual to react to the vaccine effectively. Some dogs, fortunately very few, are unable to derive full benefit from a vaccine, and so remain at risk. Second, remember that vaccines need to be topped up from time to time – so do not forget to take your dog for its regular booster injections.

Opposite: *Just good fun or the first signs of a delinquent dog? Check a pup very carefully before you agree to take it and preferably meet its parents – human and canine.*

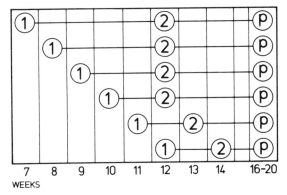

Table 5. Vaccinations: a basic scheme of timing for first (1) and second (2) doses, with suggestions for additional doses of parvovirus vaccine (P).

7 8 9 10 11 12 13 14 16–20
WEEKS

Internal parasites

There is so much nonsense written about worms in dogs that some clarification is needed to correct misapprehensions. Forget all that you have read or heard about the hazards of worms, blindness in your children and the rest of it. Follow simple rules of hygiene and common sense will prevail.

Many kinds of worms affect dogs, but only two need cause much concern in most temperate countries, including Britain: tapeworms and roundworms. They are quite distinct, have different life cycles and present no problem in control.

Tapeworms

Unless you happen to live in a country, or part of one, where hydatid cyst is a problem (it affects only two areas of Britain), there is absolutely, definitely no risk to you, your family, your neighbours and even your dog if it has a tapeworm.

Tapeworms need an intermediate host to complete their life cycle. This means that the segments full of eggs passed by your dog can be eaten until they come out of your ears and absolutely nothing will happen – unless you were to eat enough of them, in which case you would put on weight as, like all eggs, they are excellent protein! They have to be eaten by the intermediate host in which they develop into what is called the cysticercus or bladder stage. If the intermediate host is then eaten by the dog, another tapeworm will develop in the dog's gut.

The common tapeworm of the dog has the flea as its intermediate host. If you know your dog has a tapeworm and you plan treatment, include flea control in your plans as well or you will fight a losing battle. There are other tapeworms of the dog, with their own intermediate hosts such as rabbits, hares, squirrels and rodents. These are of little significance as they are not common and do no harm.

However, even though they are harmless to you and the family there is a certain amount of aesthetic objection to their presence. People do not generally like the idea of white segments squirming on the carpet, nor, even, the dried-up segments which resemble grains of rice. There are any number of tapeworm remedies available over the counter at the pet store and elsewhere, although vets themselves now prescribe newer and more effective compounds. There is even an injectable treatment.

Roundworms

There are three species of roundworm in the dog but only one of them is really important, *Toxocara canis*, because this is the one that can undergo part of its life cycle in man.

To start at the beginning (which came first, the worm or the egg?): the dog eats an egg. It has to be a special egg, a *Toxocara* egg containing an infective larva. When the egg is swallowed, it releases the infective larva in the stomach. The larva then migrates through the body and eventually ends up in the small intestine.

Here it grows into the adult and lays eggs which are passed out in the dog's faeces. The important fact to remember is that those eggs can be eaten by a dog, a baby, a child or even yourself and nothing will happen; at least, the eggs will not infect anyone or anything. They need at least two weeks in the right temperature and humidity to become infective larvae. In colder times of the year it will be several weeks, even months, before they are infective. It is to be hoped, of course, that you clear away the dog's

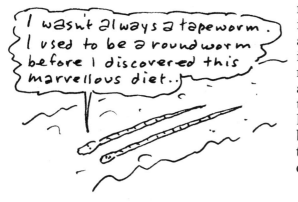

I wasn't always a tapeworm. I used to be a roundworm before I discovered this marvellous diet..

motions when they are passed in the garden or, indeed, in children's play areas. If this were standard action by dog owners it would virtually eliminate any risk to children.

But what is the risk to children? The larva of an infective egg swallowed by a human will undergo a partial migration in the body and die where it settles. In most cases the site is quite innocuous but occasionally the larva may come to rest in a fairly vital one, such as the retina. In a site like that it may do some harm, but its effects are not blindness, only partial loss of sight. This is quite serious enough, of course, and any case is one too many, but the chances of it actually happening are very small. Compare the handful of *Toxocara* cases reported each year with the thousands upon thousands killed or maimed on the roads in the same period.

Roundworm control

The incidence of roundworm in humans may not be particularly high but naturally all owners would want to reduce it to zero. One of the most useful things any dog owner can do is to worm the dog regularly.

Because puppies are extremely susceptible to roundworm and produce more eggs in their faeces than adults do, it is vital to worm pups regularly. As soon as you eliminate one lot of worms from the gut of the pup more larvae arrive from other tissues where they have been lying in wait. It is therefore necessary to worm pups at regular intervals, preferably at 6, 8, 10, 12 and 16 weeks and six months old. Your vet will advise you of suitable treatments when you take the pup for its first vaccination.

External parasites

There are a number of creepy-crawlies, even jumpy-wumpies, that try to keep a dog up to scratch. They can be very successful too. Most problems have their solution: in this case it is mass murder of the fellow travellers.

Fleas

Fleas, it has been said, are like the poor – always with us, although preferably not actually in our home. There are several species of fleas that infest dogs (and cats and man), all of which are liable to be around at any time of year if you have central heating and fitted carpets. It is not that fleas are attracted to modern luxury, just that our taste for it has provided the ideal year-round conditions for their breeding and survival.

It was different in the old days. Our grandparents could look at a dog scratching itself and know that fleas were unlikely to be the cause as it was the wrong time of year. No longer! The average owner tends to think of fleas as soon as the dog is seen to scratch. However, it is worth remembering that if fleas are present then a dog is likely to scratch many different parts of its body, rather than a single area. And if it does scratch itself the problem might be something other than fleas, unless *you* gave it the fleas in the first place.

Having established that your dog has fleas, what do you do? The trouble is that the female flea lays her eggs in those dark, dirty corners that houses never used to have until the arrival of fitted carpets and all the rest. Each female lays between 200 and 500 eggs and in the right conditions her brood can hatch and reach maturity in a mere two weeks. The potential for a population explosion is therefore horrendous and the invading army patrolling your luxurious soft carpets and furnishings must be hit very hard indeed.

The answer is to obtain a long-lasting insecticidal spray as soon as possible and apply it to your dog so that the animal is converted into a walking insecticidal strip. Some sprays are claimed to be active for at least two weeks and so if used five times at two-week intervals will make the dog insecticidal for 70 days. During that time, every baby flea that emerges from the breeding grounds, often the area between the carpet and the skirting-board, will die before it has time to suck enough blood to become adult. In this way the plague is avoided, but it is vital to treat any other animals in the household at the same time.

Flea collars are popular with some owners, but most collars have little effect when a flea population is already well established in the house. And why waste money on a popgun when a blunderbuss is clearly required? A proper insecticidal spray is the only effective way of ensuring a flea-free dog and household.

Lice

In contrast to fleas, lice lay their eggs on the animal, attaching them firmly to its hair. Lice are usually more of a problem in puppies than adult dogs; they are normally found on the ears but can occur on other parts of the body. A short-acting insecticide is often enough to control these tiny pinkish-white invaders when used at weekly intervals, but if there has been considerable irritation it may be necessary to have treatment for the sores that are likely to result.

Ear mites

Ear mites, which look like tiny greyish-white dots, live in, on or around the ears where they bite into the skin and cause exudation, inflammation and crust formation on the skin surface. The mites more commonly affect cats, although less severely, but as cats act as a reservoir of infection they should be treated at the same time as your dog.

The symptoms of an infestation are general irritation accompanied by head shaking, scratching or rubbing the ears. There is a typical dark brown wax in the

And don't come back!

ears, often with secondary bacterial and fungal infections. The breeds with drop ears are usually the worst affected as the structure of their ears encourages high humidity and a stagnant atmosphere in the ear canal.

When there are no bacterial or fungal complications, treatment is quite straightforward using insecticidal ear-drops given every three to four days to ensure that each batch of hatching eggs is killed off. However, it is important to be sure that no damage has been done to the ear canal itself and so it is wisest to have any case of suspected ear-mite infestation checked by your vet.

Sarcoptic mange

Sarcoptic mange is a skin disease caused by parasitic mites and is capable of being transmitted from dogs to man. It occurs most frequently in puppies that have become infested before they leave their mother. It is less common in adult dogs because of the more hygienic and controlled conditions in which they are normally kept. Signs of an infestation in your dog will appear in the form of skin lesions, most commonly around the eyes, muzzle or ears, spreading then to the limbs, abdomen and neck.

Children are most at risk of catching the disease from their tendency to hug the family pet, and so pick up the mites, while playing with it. If you think that your dog might have mange, check any young children in the household for skin lesions in the belly region – mites are most likely to have slipped into the gap between T-shirt or jumper and pants.

Adults do not expose themselves, at least not in that way nor when they are cuddling a pup! If the children do have lesions it is very likely that the dog, and the children, have sarcoptic mange. It is then a simple matter of choosing which to do first – taking the children to the doctor to be vetted or the dog to vet to be treated.

The female mite burrows underneath the skin, making a tunnel in which she lays her eggs. The eggs hatch and within 14 days they are adult and repeat the process. This produces intense irritation. The dog persistently scratches the lesions, the skin becomes reddened, thickened and wrinkled, a crust develops, there is loss of hair, and the dog, not surprisingly, looks mangy. There is also a characteristic smell which is easily recognized with experience, but with luck you will be spared the opportunity to gain it. For those with a poorly developed sense of smell, skin scrapings examined under the microscope will confirm the diagnosis.

Fortunately sarcoptic manage is not very common, but as the condition can be passed from dog to man (and vice versa) professional advice should be sought on treatment.

Demodectic mange

This mange is caused by another kind of mite that lives in the hair follicles or the sebaceous glands of the skin.

First the bad news. It is difficult to cure because the treatments have to be able to penetrate to the mites in the relative safety of their habitat. Now the good news. Demodectic mange is not particularly common and is not easily passed on to other dogs (and cannot be passed on to man at all). Of course, this will be no consolation if you have only one dog and it happens to be one of the unfortunate few.

The signs of this mange are bald patches, often with small pustules if there is secondary bacterial infection. There will also be small pinpoint lesions on the skin but the untrained will find them difficult to detect. If you suspect this problem in your dog you should consult the vet without delay.

Other manges

The rabbit fur mite, *Cheyletiella*, can infest cat, man, fox and dog as well – clearly a pest with catholic tastes. It produces either a scaly skin somewhat similar to dandruff (but without any loss of hair) or bald, circular, crusty lesions about 2–5 mm across. If there is hair loss in the scaly form this is usually because of self-inflicted damage through the dog scratching.

Harvest mites can lead to intense irritation, frequently between the digits of the feet. They are tiny, red creatures just visible to the naked eye and are easily eliminated with insecticides.

Ticks

Ticks are usually more worrying to the owner than to the dog. They are typically picked up on country rambles and it is only after several days of blood-sucking that the engorged parasite is discovered. A tick will usually drop off of its own accord when it has had its fill, but most owners will want to get rid of it as soon as they discover that their pride and joy is ambling around with a miniature vampire attached.

Careful examination of the beast will reveal the head with its mouthparts firmly embedded in the dog's skin. If the tick is not removed intact, the mouthparts will be left in the skin with a good chance of a septic wound. The best way to deal with the problem is to apply surgical spirit and firmly grasp the tick with tweezers as far forward as possible. Pull *very* gently until it looses its hold.

7. First aid

Unfortunately, accidents occur in even the best-regulated families. And when disaster strikes, as it is bound to sooner or later, you may find yourself miles from home, probably already coping with another disaster and almost certainly without this book. You would probably not have enough time to consult the book even if you did have it with you – either that or you cannot find your glasses. Of course, your bad luck will be nothing compared to that of your dog, so prepare for emergency procedures now (and memorize your vet's telephone number).

The run-of-the-mill problems covered in this chapter are most easily dealt with under the various parts of the body, such as the mouth, ears and so on, or in general if they can arise anywhere.

The head

Foreign bodies in the mouth

Technically, a foreign body is something from outside the animal which is lodged in some part of the animal's anatomy. A thorn in the flesh is one example of a foreign body. A client who does not pay the bill is a thorn in the flesh to a vet, but that is quite a different thing altogether.

The most common foreign body in the dog's mouth is a bone or stick which breaks when being held across the mouth between the upper and lower teeth on both sides. It then becomes jammed against the hard palate between the upper molars. Usually the owner is only aware of the dog pawing frantically at its mouth, almost going demented; there is often increased salivation. A look into the mouth may not reveal the problem, either, stuck as it is in a difficult place to see.

The immediate reaction is to try to pull the bone or stick out, but beware. The space between the teeth on either side of the mouth is usually wider at the back than the front in most breeds and if you pull the foreign body forwards it will only become more firmly fixed. The simple answer is to *push* the object towards the *back* of the mouth, but this is easier said than done. There is also the risk that it may be replaced by a second – some part of your hand!

As you probably want to keep your hand intact, the most sensible thing to do, if you cannot dislodge the object quickly and simply, is take the dog to your vet without further delay. It will not only save your hand but calm the dog down if it is over-excited. This is because the vet is likely to give it a sedative injection before dealing with the problem.

Another common foreign body in centres of domesticity is the good old needle and thread. Some wives never seem to know where they come from, but you can be sure that even if your dog's mouth is not magnetic it will find the occasional stray needle, threaded or unthreaded. The needle may be visible when the mouth is opened. Visible or not, resist any temptation to pull the loose thread (if present) unless it is double and you can grasp both ends. That thread may be useful for the vet when he looks for the needle.

A fairly common problem in the angling enthusiast's home is the errant fishing hook. Despite all those stories about the one that got away, these hooks are designed to stay put. If the barb is showing on one side of the wound and the ring end on the other, all that needs to be done is to break the hook in between the two ends and pull out the part that is still embedded. This is easier said than done unless the animal is sedated, and as most barbs can quickly become deeply embedded as well as extremely painful you should see that your dog is taken for prompt veterinary treatment.

Choking

Choking is usually caused by a foreign body but occasionally by a swollen tongue or spasm of the throat. Any foreign body needs to be removed

promptly. If you are unable to do so yourself, get the dog to the vet as soon as possible.

Owners who hear gagging often suspect that 'something is stuck in the throat' but on checking the dog discover that it is still eating. If the dog is swallowing its food then it is unlikely to have a blocked throat! On the other hand, this may mean that the object, if there was one there at all, has now been swallowed. Owners are usually very worried then. Fearing the worst, they think there may be a blockage down the oesophagus far beyond the reach of a questing finger. If the dog swallows food and keeps it down for a little while, forget your worry. A blocked oesophagus means that food comes straight up again, just like a Yo-Yo, without any pause. There can still be trouble in store for all you know, but that is a different matter.

Foreign bodies in the eye

If the foreign body is embedded in the eye itself, go to the vet immediately. Specks of dust or dirt, on the other hand, caught either on the eye or under the eyelid, can be removed by using the corner of a handkerchief. After removing any foreign body from your dog's eye, check occasionally for signs of soreness or inflammation and if any develop make an appointment for treatment sooner rather than later.

Foreign bodies in the ear

The first time this happens the owner thinks that the dog has an acute attack of earache. It has probably been out for a walk or in the garden not long ago, and now it suddenly goes demented, in acute pain, holding its head on one side and/or shaking the head and ears. The symptoms are unmistakable and most commonly occur in dogs with drop ears.

There is nothing, but nothing, you can do to help. The chances are that there is an awned grass seed down the ear canal. It is now obvious that this is most likely to be in the summer or autumn. If it was picked up in your garden it is also obvious that you have not kept up with your gardening.

There is a great temptation to put oil into the ear. This is an age-old remedy for all earaches and would be fine if your dog really had earache, which is a middle ear infection. Avoid the temptation and go to the vet instead. The dog will generally need sedation, if not anaesthesia, before the vet can look down the ear, find the grass seed (so much easier without any oil) and then grasp it. An impossible task in a dog that is moving its head about and even more so if the rest of the dog is on the move as well.

The seed is usually picked up on the ear flap and travels up the inside of the flap, sharp end first, into the ear canal. There, it awaits the vet's special crocodile forceps with which he grasps it and withdraws it to the outside, rather like a conjuror producing a rabbit out of an empty top hat.

Inflamed ears

When the ears are inflamed, the skin is red and there is often a discharge that

owners want to wipe away. If you are going to take the dog to the vet then do not do any cleaning up in the ear itself. Indeed, you should never clean any more of the ears than you can actually see, so keep an eye on the end of the cotton bud that you are now using to wipe away this discharge – the end that you are putting down the ear, not the end you are holding. If you are going to clean deep down the ear, never use anything smaller than your elbow. In other words, do not do it.

Coughs

As coughs emerge from the head they are covered in this section, although they could just as easily be covered under problems of the body as coughing is symptomatic of a number of diseases that need treatment by your vet. As these include kennel cough, in which loss of appetite is unusual, it is difficult to suggest a course of action as long as the dog is eating. Coughing can also be associated with heart disease, which is why a persistent one is cause enough to go to the vet.

Strokes

A stroke is due to cerebral haemorrhage, generally the result of trauma, such as a road accident, but occasionally without apparent cause. It occurs mainly in old age. There may sometimes be loss of consciousness and a degree of paralysis.

If the mucous membranes of the mouth and the tongue are not blue or purple, keep the dog quiet and warm, give it a warm drink of, say, sweet tea and get it to the vet as soon as is convenient for all three of you. If the mucous membranes and tongue *are* blue, get the vet to visit your house if at all possible.

The body

Heart problems

Heart problems must be distinguished from problems of the heart, which are covered in the next chapter. The heart can be a problem in young dogs but mostly affects the relatively old dog.

The only heart problem that involves first aid is a heart attack. An owner can sometimes mistake an attack for a fit, especially the first time. The dog may collapse, lie on its side and pant with forelegs rigid. There is obvious distress and frequently loss of consciousness. The tongue and the mucous membranes are often purple or even blue.

Lie the dog on its right side, ensure that the airways are clear and there is a plentiful supply of fresh air. Consult the vet as soon as possible.

Constipation

A dog's motions should be quite firm, but some owners tend to think that a really firm motion is synonymous with constipation. Providing the motion is able to be passed with reasonable ease, the dog is not constipated.

A firm motion is desirable as it is more likely to keep the anal glands emptied. Occasionally a dog may apparently strain to pass a motion and have a foreign body just inside the anus that is too large and painful to pass through. If the object is not passed it will not take long for real constipation to occur.

The first-aid treatment for constipation is liquid paraffin, an inert mineral oil that is excreted at the tail end in the same form as it was taken in. It simply oils the works but has no laxative effect. Give 0.1–0.5 fl oz (3–14 ml) by mouth, three times a day for one or two days. The dose depends on size of dog rather than severity of symptoms.

Diarrhoea

Although diarrhoea is a symptom of several diseases, it can also occur simply as the result of an upset digestive system. If the animal is bright, alert and the motion is not absolutely like water in consistency, try modifying the diet until the dog's digestion has settled and the motion has recovered its shape. Lightly boiled or scrambled egg with boiled rice is the order of the day. If the motions are watery or bloody, or if the dog is vomiting as well, do not waste time. See your vet (do not forget to take the dog along too).

Other problems

These problems are found in many or any parts of the body.

Bites

Dogs are usually bitten by other dogs; newspapers are still waiting for the 'man bites dog' story. Dogs may be flea-bitten too, in more ways than one, but that is not the kind of bite requiring immediate first aid.

A dog bite is usually a penetrating wound because of the shape of the canine teeth. Its depth depends on the size of the dog that bit and also on that of the recipient. If the biter used its incisors rather than the canines, the wound will be shallow and more of a tear. Where a canine has gone through the skin it is likely that there will be another hole opposite it from the opposite tooth. A bite in the legs may penetrate joints and sever blood vessels and tendons. In that case prompt veterinary attention will obviously be necessary.

Less severe wounds should be cleaned using one teaspoonful of salt to 10 fl oz (280 ml) of warm water, cotton wool and great care. Do not wash dirt and debris into the wound but clean up around it. Hair may have been introduced into the hole in the process of biting. This should be lifted out gently, which is quite easy when it is still attached to the hair follicle, and if necessary clipped away. You can count on the fact that the bite wounds will be infected. Once you have done your bit, dash down to the vet for an antibiotic injection.

Burns and scalds

These are not to be confused with hot dogs. The burns most likely to occur are thermal, caused by flames or radiant heat, or contact with scalding liquids or electric current. Because of their inquisitive nature and often clumsy behaviour, puppies and younger dogs are most likely to be at risk. Electrical burns can be very serious because of the associated shock, which is why you should discourage a young pup from investigating any chewable flex.

Immediately after a burn or scald, try to cool the area with cold water or cold compresses. Pain usually passes off in an hour or two in mild cases when air is excluded, which is easier said than done. Prevent the dog licking or gnawing the burn, if necessary with an Elizabethan collar. Avoid putting Vaseline or grease of any sort on the area. If you vet needs to treat the wound a barrier like that is distinctly unhelpful.

Apart from thermal burns, there are also burns from acids and alkalis. If either of these occur they should be neutralized with sodium bicarbonate for acids and vinegar for alkalis. Burns with strong phenol (carbolic acid) can be neutralized with surgical or methylated spirit. After neutralizing any chemical burn wash the wound with mild soap and water. If in any doubt go to the vet once you have given first aid.

Fractures

Fractures can be the result of an obvious incident, such as a road accident, where the impact is clearly sufficient to break bones. They can also arise from quite minor knocks and bumps.

If a long bone has an uncomplicated, simple fracture there will be freedom of movement from the fracture site which might well be confused with a joint if it were not in the wrong place. The area is usually swollen and moving the legs tends to produce a kind of grating, called crepitus, as the ends of the broken bone rub against each other. A compound fracture is one where there is a break in the skin made by the bone, often protruding through it. Not all fractures are so obvious, however, and if you suspect that your dog might have a broken bone then note the following procedure.

The first objective with any fracture is to immobilize it, which reduces pain. Providing the position of the break permits bandaging for a sufficient distance on both sides of the fracture to prevent movement, apply a splint. Due to the way dogs are constructed it is not possible to splint the femur (thigh bone) as the top half or third of it is bordered by the abdomen.

To apply a splint, pad the limb with enough cotton wool to prevent chafing by the splint – use a handy length of wood or metal for this part – and bandage firmly into position. Under *no* circumstances should this be regarded as anything more than a temporary measure and as soon as the dog is fit to travel take it along for veterinary attention.

Treatment may take one of several forms, such as external splinting in plaster of Paris or one of its modern alternatives, internal fixation or even

intramedullary pinning. Once the dog is fixed up with one or other of those, it will get around with remarkable ease. After all, it is blessed with built-in crutches and can get around very well on three legs. One Pomeranian walked erect on both hind legs until an operation for lameness in them. It then walked on its two front legs.

Fits

Fits range from the extremely mild to severe convulsions; either kind may occur without warning. They are invariably distressing to the owner and not exactly beneficial for the dog, either. The very mild type may consist of nothing more than a blank staring into space with pupils widely dilated, lasting from a split second to a minute or more.

The more severe grades have various degrees of uncontrollable spasms, collapse to the floor, shaking of legs or even a running movement while lying on the side. There may well be champing of the jaws with excessive salivation. This leads to a degree of frothing round the mouth.

These fits last anything from a minute or two to much longer. Quiet and a darkened room are the best treatment at this stage but contact the vet as soon as possible. In the meantime remove the dog's collar and ensure that it cannot injure itself on nearby objects. Anticonvulsants, which the vet may prescribe, are very helpful and the ones now available are without excessive sedation as a side-effect.

Poisoning

It is easy to say that you should avoid using poisons unless you have to, but every house will contain one or two – a jar of slug bait, for example, or a spare bottle of antifreeze for the car (which dogs find sweet-tasting). The vital point is to ensure that no marauding dog (especially yours) or cat can get at them and to be prepared for emergency treatment. Every household with a pet should have a store of washing soda crystals for use as an emetic. Dosage for the soda is a piece about the size of a walnut for a Labrador, smaller or larger according to size of dog. It does not do any harm to give a double dose, so err on the liberal side. The dog usually vomits in about two or three minutes.

Check the vomit to see whether the suspect poison is actually there. Then rush the animal to your vet.

Snake bites

Early treatment is essential if your dog is bitten by a poisonous snake and you should *not* try to suck the poison out, whatever others may say.

If the snake bite is on a limb, the immediate action is to prevent the venom from travelling to vital organs via the bloodstream by means of a tourniquet about 2 in (5 cm) above the bite. The tourniquet must not completely stop the circulation but simply reduce it. After 15 minutes the tourniquet should be relaxed for a minute or two and then reapplied. Restrict movement, keep the dog quiet and get it to the vet.

Hypothermia

Hypothermia is an extreme loss of body heat caused by over-exposure to cold. In mild cases put the dog into an environment of 68–79 °F (20–26 °C) and massage. Frosting makes the skin turn pale, but later it reddens with heat, pain and swelling. There may be loss of hair and peeling. In severe cases there may be frostbite: the swelling will be very painful and the skin will not warm up because the tissue is already dead. Prompt veterinary treatment is now indicated.

Heat exhaustion

This is most likely to occur in hot and humid weather when, for example, a dog has been left in an inadequately ventilated car. The victim will be in obvious distress, breathing rapidly and probably drooling. Take immediate action by dousing the dog with cold water, preferably in a bath packed with ice. Then call the vet.

Cuts

Cuts longer than an inch or two will nearly always require suturing to minimize scarring, promote healing and control infection.

First aid in such cases is best limited to assessing the extent of the damage. Leave any cleaning up to the professional expertise of the vet. However, when a cut is bleeding copiously you will need to do something more, and quickly.

The principle was described on page 77 and here is the chance to put it to the test. If the blood is bright red and spurting out, an artery has been severed. This means that the blood is travelling *from* the heart *to* the tissue, so apply a tourniquet between the cut and the heart. With darker, more venous blood the tourniquet should be applied between the cut and the limb extremity because the blood is travelling *from* the tissues *to* the heart. One way of checking if you have got it right is to see whether the tourniquet staunches the bleeding. If it does, leave it alone; if not, then either the tourniquet is not tight enough or you have it in the wrong place.

Naturally, you need to go to the vet as soon as possible.

Dermatitis

There are few cases of dermatitis that actually *need* first-aid treatment. There are hardly any first-aid treatments that are likely to help, anyway, because the majority of cases need a diagnosis of the primary cause before a remedy can be effected.

The main problem with dermatitis is the animal's insatiable desire to scratch or nibble, and the best first aid you can give is to prevent this self-inflicted damage. The area of irritation is scratched by a hind leg, perhaps? Put a sock on it so the claws are covered. It is being nibbled? Put a bucket or Elizabethan collar on to stop it. Just in case you misunderstand, make a hole in the bottom of a plastic bucket big enough to pass over the dog's head and fix it to the collar. That is more pleasant than just putting a bucket over its head.

Accidents

Most people's immediate reaction to an accident is to call out the vet. This is not the best thing to do. Instead, telephone the vet, warn him (or her) that you are on your way with an injured dog and explain the extent of the damage as far as you can (cuts, possible fractures, a scald, etc.).

Do things this way round and the dog will be receiving treatment much sooner than if the vet has to drive all the way to you, apply temporary first aid and then drive all the way back with the injured animal for full emergency treatment on his premises. Most accident injuries need to go to surgery for suturing, at the least, and while you are on your way the vet can be preparing for your arrival.

Not all accidents involving dogs take place on the roads, but many do. Nor are they always serious, indeed in some cases the car may come off worse than the dog – just hope that it was not a Rolls Royce. But all accidents should be treated as if they were serious because even a superficial knock may prove much more damaging than at first appears. Keep the dog quiet and warm to minimize the effects of shock, check for signs of injury, apply first aid if necessary and then head for the vet.

If the dog is seriously injured and in discomfort – and it may well be after a typical road accident – slide it on to a flat board as a temporary stretcher. An alternative is to use a blanket held at all four corners. One problem with an injured dog is that your good intentions may be misconstrued. You know you are trying to help, but the dog may regard you as a threat when it is in pain. In that situation it will bite first and lick its wounds afterwards, so for safety's sake you should apply a tape muzzle. Not that you can expect to have a tape or bandage with you, necessarily – a little ingenuity will be needed to overcome that problem.

It was much easier in the old days when you asked a passing lady to let you have one of her stockings. The asking was not any easier, just the ease of removing a pair of stockings instead of a pair of tights.

8. Sex or celibacy?

One of the advantages of having a pet, as well as children, is the opportunity for the children to learn something about the facts of life in a matter-of-fact way. It is just as easy to learn from the dog as it is from the birds and the bees. Anyway, although birds may be better than nothing for those living in flats where no other form of pet is permitted, bees are hardly suitable pets!

Not that a programme of canine procreation should be embarked on willy-nilly; there are enough unwanted dogs as it is. Breeding should be planned and limited. There is no excuse for unwanted litters even if there is an accidental mating – although, as far as the dog and bitch are concerned, it was no accident!

The male dog

Anatomy

The external genitalia consist of the prepuce containing the penis and the scrotum containing the two testicles. The dog is so constructed that when it mates with a bitch the base of the penis swells enormously and the dog 'ties' to the female.

When the dog has an erection the penis is not all that more rigid than in its non-erect state, due to the bone in it (as described earlier on page 79). Some owners are inclined to be worried when their dog is observed to have tied and attempts to dismount from the bitch. As a result of the tie, the dog ends up tail-to-tail with the bitch with its penis doubling back on itself.

Such contortions are regarded by us as a physically impossible position, yet another example of anthropomorphism no doubt, and owners may think it is an emergency situation. It is perfectly natural and if nature is left to take its course, all will be well.

Puberty

The onset of puberty in the male dog is variable and the smaller breeds tend to reach sexual maturity earlier. It is usually at about 5–12 months of age.

With that degree of variation it is not surprising that there is also variation in the timing of the descent of the testicles into the scrotum. Some books describe the testicles as descending into the scrotum at, or shortly after, birth, but it is more usual for them to be in the abdomen at birth and descend over the next few days, reaching the scrotum between 10 and 14 days of age. At that age, however, the scrotum does not hang down as it does in the adult, but is just a small sac lying close to the abdomen. It may be

difficult to palpate the testicles in that area in the first two to four months of life as it is usual for fat to be laid down around them. By six months of age most dogs have a well-developed scrotum and there are two obvious testicles within.

So do not be too worried if your dog is apparently without his full complement of parts. They are usually somewhere about. It does not really matter unless he is a perfect specimen and likely to be made up to a champion in the show ring.

The male sexual urge

The majority of male dogs spend a happy life without promiscuity of any kind. Perhaps it is a matter of what they have never had they never miss. However, the novice owner is inclined to think that if tom cats are invariably neutered, then the same thing must apply to the dog.

In fact, routine orchidectomy (a rather nicer technical term than castration as it is not so emotive and might be freely translated as being deflowered!) in cats is more than a means to increase the living standards of the veterinary profession.

Entire (which means fully equipped) male cats have a greater urge to fight others, are inclined to wander and so be at more risk of being struck by motor vehicles and invariably spray their smelly urine on strategically placed objects around the house. The incentive to obviate these problems is clear.

The male dog does not present the same antisocial characteristics and unless it is both over-sexed and allowed to roam (how can you confine a tom cat to the garden?), it is no more likely than a bitch to be hit by a car. This is not to say that the average male does not get the urge when a bitch is in heat in the immediate vicinity, but the dog is usually manageable and not intent on rape at all costs.

Coping with the over-sexed male

Most puppies will become aware of a new dimension to life at the onset of puberty. There is nothing unusual about this. It occurs in the human male as well (and some never grow out of it).

Sexual drive comes from the male

hormone testosterone, produced by the testicles. Once this hormone begins to course through the bloodstream the male characteristics appear. In man it is the development of a beard or the onset of shaving. In the dog it is the cocking of the leg. This procedure would seem to have some evolutionary justification in that urine can be directed more accurately against a tree or other object with the leg cocked than in a squatting posture.

Urine marking is advertising the dog's availability to passing bitches, and who can deny the power of advertising? Unfortunately, some dogs find a certain pleasure (at least, it would be certain if they were permitted to get away with it) in clasping a passing leg, canine or human, and using it to gratify their urge to masturbate. Firm correction at the outset is usually all that is needed, though it may take a little time for the lesson to sink in. Such reluctance is possibly due to one of Mother Nature's built-in safeguards for the survival of the species. If all males gave up after the first few rebuffs, few of us would probably be here today. In any event, there is no cause to embark on an urgent surgical exercise to correct what may be only a passing phase in the dog's development.

However, there *are* some individuals so over-sexed that they would escape from a padlocked heavy-duty nylon bag ten feet underwater, muzzled and with all four limbs firmly roped together, if they detected a bitch in heat within three miles. An eight-foot fence would neither keep such an animal in your garden nor out of the bitch's. Such dogs may well benefit from orchidectomy (although they themselves would hardly describe it as a benefit) and give you peace of mind, not to mention peace of mind for all those who own bitches in the neighbourhood.

The operation is not as traumatic as owners fear. The dog is admitted for only a day in most cases, or even part of the day. It will have none of the human hang-ups about operations and will not come to after the anaesthetic thinking 'I've had an operation. I must feel terrible.' Neither, fortunately, will it realize that its brief spell under the scalpel is going to have an effect that most men would dread.

Side-effects of orchidectomy

Apart from the obvious effects of the operation, there are no other side-effects that cannot be overcome. The age at which the operation is performed may well have a bearing on the incidence of any that do occur.

The opinion widely held by vets is that castration before puberty is more likely to be detrimental. Obesity is a common sequel to surgery before puberty, as well as an apparent lack of character development frequently leading to indolence. It is also possible that the dog may become more vicious or, even worse, attractive to other male dogs (but there is no evidence that these two are in any way connected). Waiting until after puberty minimizes the chances of these undesirable things happening.

Even if there is a tendency to put on weight after the operation, this is only because of improved efficiency in converting food into flesh – and fat. Every dog that is castrated should be weighed *after* the operation (if you do it beforehand there is an almost immediate loss of weight!) and at fixed intervals of, say, 7–14 days. Plot the weights on a chart with a bold line across it showing the starting weight. Ignore the week-to-week variations that are bound to occur until there is a definite trend upwards on the chart. When this happens, cut down the food offered by 10 per cent until the body weight is back to the starting level. Adjust the ration as necessary and the maintenance level is established.

Cryptorchids

A cryptorchid dog has one or more (usually less than three!) testicles retained within the abdomen. The affliction may well be hereditary and in Britain Kennel Club rules preclude the dog from being shown. Breeding from such an animal is clearly not on. Furthermore, there is a potential danger that such retained testicles may become cancerous. It is generally advised that they be removed before six years of age not only to reduce the risk of cancer in the testicles themselves but also the possibility of its spread to other tissues.

The bitch

Anatomy

Each bitch comes into the world with a built-in set of two ovaries, uterus, cervix, vagina and vulva. That is a simplification but more than adequate for our purposes, although we must not forget the mammary glands.

As far as you are concerned, the only observable parts are the vulva and teats. Keep an eye on both from time to time, for reasons that we shall go into in due course. The ovaries are the source of female hormones in much the same way as male hormones are derived from the testicles. Other hormones secreted by glands elsewhere in the body interact with those of the ovaries.

The oestrous cycle

The average bitch comes into oestrus, or heat, every six months once she reaches sexual maturity. Some have a shorter or longer interval and others that have irregular cycles. In the smaller breeds a bitch usually comes into heat for the first time when she is six to eight months old. In the larger breeds it could be as late as at a year of age or even later.

The first sign of the beginning of the heat is swelling of the vulva. It is obvious that unless you know how large (or small) the vulva is *before* the heat starts, you can hardly tell whether there is any enlargement. By the time the bitch is six months old, start regular checks to be sure you do not miss it. Shortly after the vulval enlargement you will see a blood-stained discharge from the vulva. This is the beginning of *pro-oestrus*, the stage leading up to oestrus proper.

Pro-oestrus lasts an average of 9 days but may vary with the individual bitch from 2 to 28 days. Some bitches may not actually bleed at all, in which case they are said to have a silent heat. It must be stressed that the bleeding is *not* a menstruation. That is a characteristic of primates (and I do not mean the Archbishop of Canterbury), which are the only animals to menstruate. Although some bitches may have a heavy 'show', most do not shed much blood but more of a watery, bloody discharge.

The end of the bleeding is the sign of onset of oestrus itself. It is now that the bitch is most likely to accept a dog. On average oestrus lasts nine days, although the readiness of the bitch to be mated is often much less than that. Some bitches will accept a dog on one day only, others on several days. The male dog will often show interest for longer than the bitch.

It must now be clear that the duration of both pro-oestrus and oestrus varies. As a general guide the total combined duration is usually 18 days. The shorter one is, the longer the other, by and large, but like all sweeping generalizations there are exceptions to prove the rule.

Oestrus is followed by a period of metoestrus if ovulation has occurred but no pregnancy. Metoestrus lasts about 90 days. This is followed by a period of anoestrus ('an-' being Greek for without), when the bitch is sexually inactive.

During pro-oestrus, oestrus and metoestrus the ovaries produce hormones of one kind or another. Until ovulation they produce oestrogens and afterwards progesterone. In anoestrus the ovaries are completely inactive and produce no hormones at all. If the balance of these hormones with others in the body is disturbed for any reason there can be detrimental effects upon health. For example, pyometra (see page 85), false pregnancy (page 118) and some skin problems are caused by hormonal upsets.

Controlling oestrus

If the average bitch is in heat twice a year, this means virtual purdah for 6 weeks out of 52. If it is not kept secure you are likely to have all the neighbourhood males on your doorstep and even the patter of tiny paws.

At the first sign of dogs being interested in your bitch, therefore, stop taking her out. Some enthusiastic owners who feel that exercise is very important have been known to carry their bitch into the car to avoid laying a trail, drive to a remote spot and have a walk in peace and tranquility. At four o'clock in the morning. The usual 7–8 a.m. doggy parade subsequently has an exhilarating time following a trail that leads only to frustration.

It is understandable to put up with such inconvenience if you ultimately intend to breed from your bitch, or you may be fortunate enough to have a large but very secure garden. On the other hand, if you are in neither camp and life threatens to become impossible there are two basic options open to you. The first is surgical removal of the ovaries and uterus (ovariohysterectomy or spaying) and, secondly, chemical (hormonal) control of the oestrus cycle either to prevent oestrus or stop it once it starts.

Ovariohysterectomy

The indulgent owner often wants a bitch to have a litter of puppies before embarking upon the irrevocable step of terminating her ability to procreate. This desire is due to a misguided idea that it will leave her fulfilled. Put all such ideas behind you. If you want her to have puppies because you genuinely desire to be a dog breeder, fine. Otherwise, you should forget it.

Of all the methods of oestrus prevention in bitches, this is probably the best. It is a once-and-for-all, permanent and routine operation in almost every veterinary practice. There will always be differences of opinion on the relative merits of surgery versus chemical control, as there are on the ideal time to operate. Some vets advocate spaying at six months of age; others encourage waiting until after the first heat. Your vet will be happy to discuss the best option for your dog.

Side-effects of spaying

The reason for not operating on the prepuberal bitch is that doing so may lead

to the risk of an 'infantile vulva'. The prepuberal bitch has not finished growing at the time the operation is carried out and as the dog grows the vulva grows with it, whereas a bitch that has come into heat will have an enlarged vulva during the heat which never quite goes back to the size it was initially. It tends to protrude more than the vulva that has not been through a heat, because it is larger.

In a bitch that is spayed before reaching puberty, however, the vulva may not grow to the same extent and instead end up in a deep fold of skin with a consequential risk of dermatitis. The intermittent licking of the affected part may not be too irritating for you (unlike the bitch) but it can be embarrassing when guests come for tea. Spaying the mature bitch is also alleged to reduce the risk and severity of obesity when compared to those spayed before puberty.

On balance, there is much to be said for spaying a bitch four months or so after the start of the last heat, aiming for removal of the ovaries when the bitch is in anoestrus and not producing hormones. In this way the risk of hormonal imbalance is reduced.

It is alleged by some that spaying at any age can affect temperament, leading to a lack of character and even neurotic behaviour. Some who hold these views are not being as objective as they might be; perhaps they are even neurotic themselves. The same characteristics alleged to be related to spaying can be observed in entire bitches as well. As for obesity, that can be controlled in the same way as for the castrated male (see page 115).

Chemical oestrus control

There are two basic methods of chemical control: those given by injection and those given by mouth. Both involve hormonal treatments using man-made and more potent derivatives of the natural progesterone.

The first kind to become available were injectable. Although effective, the treatment can have side-effects that impair health or subsequent intentional breeding. The drawback of the injection method is that each jab lasts for some time and unfortunately the exact length of time is not always predictable. This means that if there *are* side-effects it is not possible to find and remove the remains of the previous jab.

The more recently developed oral form is safer in that it has to be given daily for several days because the compound is excreted from the body quite quickly. On the other hand, it has to be given at the right time at the start of oestrus. This presents a problem for the novice or unobservant owner who does not notice pro-oestrus until a few days into the heat. It also presents a problem if the bitch is not obviously in heat and is missed by the experienced owner. In these circumstances the owner may *think* the treatment is working, whereas in reality it has not had time to do so and all that is happening is the normal cessation of bleeding. If that is the case, and the owner's vigilance is let slide, pregnancy might unwittingly ensue.

False pregnancy

Having just touched on the subject of pregnancy, it may be appropriate to look at a complex condition described as false pregnancy, before going on to the real thing.

False pregnancy is a result of hormonal changes, some of which might almost be described as fairly normal and often spontaneously reversible. Others are obviously more serious and need therapy. The simplest form is where the abdomen becomes noticeably distended and the bitch's appetite increases, shortly after the end of oestrus. This may cause consternation on the part of the owner who is positive that no dog had managed to get at his pride and joy and finds it difficult to accept that the Second Coming could be in the form of a canine. In any case, there is no sign of a bright star in the East as yet. The owner of a mated bitch is going to experience consternation later, when the expected certainty of a litter does not materialize. In fact it disappears overnight together with the abdominal distension seven weeks after ovulation and/or mating.

A second type of false pregnancy is the unexpected onset of all the signs of

impending birth. The bitch is restless, reluctant to go out for walks (or even into the garden) and starts making a bed. It may take an object such as a soft toy or slipper into its bed and treat it as though it were a pup. Some bitches even start to produce milk.

Treatment is possible in all cases but may not be necessary in the milder forms, although there is no harm in asking the vet to check. If there is lactation, treatment is very desirable and as soon as possible.

Courting, marriage and honeymoon

Mating is a natural process, which does not mean that any dog will mate any bitch (although it is fairly likely if given the opportunity) nor any bitch accept any dog. Basically, they accept whom they want to accept. Indeed, the better the pedigree and perfection of the bitch, the more likely she is to spurn your selected stud dog and accept any passing mongrel.

The first question most potential breeders ask is 'when do we start breeding?' The question is unlikely to relate to a stud male, as the owners will usually first try their hand at breeding bitches. However, it is considered useful to let a potential stud dog work (if that is the right word) before it is a year old to give it some experience, but no litters that result will be very valuable until the stud has some prizes in the show ring tucked under its collar. In contrast, the family male which was discouraged from showing its sexual agility in the early stages of puberty may well be inhibited from gratifying its urges as a result of conditioned behaviour.

The time for first mating of the novice bitch is not so straightforward. It is usual to avoid the first heat unless it is very late in onset and time is running out. Aim for mating between 12 and 18 months of age. The potential breeder tends to put off the first litter until there is little left to achieve in the show ring, but if the intention is to put it off until the bitch is over two and a half years of age, please do not. There is a risk of lowered fertility in bitches where the first mating is put off until three to four years old.

When to mate

There are those who are told that a bitch should be mated at about the tenth or eleventh day of the oestrous period and treat it as an immovable feast. This is generally based on a nine-day (bleeding) pro-oestrus with acceptance one or two days after bleeding stops. Obviously, it all depends when bleeding stops as to the best time for mating.

There is little doubt that Mother Nature, left to her own devices, will seldom fail to find the optimum time. Not very long ago it was the usual practice to send a bitch to the stud several days before she was due to stop bleeding. She would be introduced to the dog and adjust to the change of environment so that when she was ready and willing in a physiological sense to accept the dog, she was ready and willing in a practical way as well.

That is a rare occurrence with many breeders these days. It is more likely to be a one-day trip there and back with a soupçon of sex thrown in the middle. If the bitch will not stand for the dog, then she will be held ready for the rape that follows. Fortunately, there *are* caring stud owners still. They are worth finding as long as they have the type of dog and the blood line you want.

The mating

Ovulation generally occurs about 24–72 hours after the end of bleeding and may be staggered over several hours or even days. The eggs live for six days or more without being fertilized so it should not be too difficult getting a normal bitch pregnant with a fertile male. The readiness of a bitch to stand can often be detected by the owner. The vulva becomes less turgid, the bleeding has stopped and when the skin above the vulva is stroked the bitch will expose the vulva by moving the tail sideways and upwards.

During service there are three fractions of the ejaculation. The first part is watery and contains no sperms. These are in the second fraction. The third fraction facilitates sperm transport up the genital tract but is not essential for conception. The tie was referred to earlier in this chapter (see page 112). It is not essential to fertile mating but is a desirable feature as it is more likely to lead to pregnancy. It lasts anything from 5 to 50 minutes as a general rule, but may be longer.

Mésalliance or mismating

Occasionally even a bitch belonging to a responsible owner will accidentally escape from premises that are regarded as secure as Fort Knox. Even more likely, an intruding canine Casanova manages to penetrate not only the outer perimeter defences.

There is no doubt of the action to be

taken if your bitch is known to have been mated, whether a tie resulted or not. If a litter is undesirable, for whatever reason, get down to the vet in the next 72 hours. Pregnancy may be averted at 96 hours, but you might as well make it sooner rather than later. Treatment (by an injection) is usually successful but has the disadvantage of leaving your bitch in heat for a further 21 days. Still, you already knew that prevention is better than cure.

Pregnancy

The dog has a gestation period of 63 days. If only all bitches knew that, life would be so much easier for owners and vets alike. The truth is that a birth within seven days either side is still within the normal range, so do not be too worried if your bitch starts whelping at 56 days or has not begun when the sixty-third day is over.

It is easier to forecast the date of whelping in a bitch mated on only one day than over several days. Nevertheless, it is customary to calculate the date of whelping from first service. Table 6 (page 122) will help you to work this out.

Pregnancy diagnosis

There are no urine tests for a canine pregnancy and the testing kits used for women are of no value to the dog owner. There is no quick and easy way of putting your mind at rest over whether your bitch is pregnant or not, nor whether you will get your money's worth for the stud fee.

The only way is to take the dog for an examination, but first check with the vet that the dog is at the right stage. In the smaller breeds it is often possible for the vet to palpate the small swellings on the uterus 21 days after mating, but this is not so easy in the larger breeds. It is therefore the general rule in many practices to carry out pregnancy diagnosis between 26 and 31 days after mating when the uterine swellings are a little larger. If the examination is delayed beyond that stage the uterus gradually becomes enlarged along its length instead of around the developing foetuses, thus rendering diagnosis almost impossible until around the fiftieth day, by which time pregnancy will probably be obvious anyway.

Other signs of pregnancy

Teats
About 28 days into a pregnancy the teats may become reddened (if the skin pigment permits, of course), enlarged and erectile, especially in a bitch in its first pregnancy.

Vaginal discharge
During the fifth week of pregnancy there is usually a thick mucous discharge which persists until shortly before birth. It may be only a small amount on the hairs of the vulva but can sometimes be hanging in strings. Absence of a discharge will invariably mean that the bitch is not pregnant. If the discharge does not start until the seventh week the

Table 6. Gestation: a guide to dates on which whelping is due, on average 63 days after mating. A variation of seven days either way is still within the normal range.

MATING		WHELPING		MATING		WHELPING	
January	1	March	5	July	2	September	3
	8		12		9		10
	15		19		16		17
	22		26		23		24
	29	April	2		30	October	1
February	5		9	August	6		8
	12		16		13		15
	19		23		20		22
	26		30		27		29
March	5	May	7	September	3	November	5
	12		14		10		12
	19		21		17		19
	26		28		24		26
April	2	June	4	October	1	December	3
	9		11		8		10
	16		18		15		17
	23		25		22		24
	30	July	2		29		31
May	7		9	November	5	January	7
	14		16		12		14
	21		23		19		21
	28		30		26		28
June	4	August	6	December	3	February	4
	11		13		10		11
	18		20		17		18
	25		27		24		25
					31	March	4

bitch probably has a false pregnancy that is about to end.

Behaviour
There are changes in behaviour and temperament in some but not all bitches and their presence or absence cannot be regarded as aids to pregnancy diagnosis. Bitches do not have morning sickness.

Feeding during pregnancy

Increased appetite and thirst midway through a pregnancy are usual but they are unlikely in the first four or five weeks. Providing the bitch is not too fat, increase the amount of food offered to satisfy her appetite.

If the bitch is carrying a small litter

she may not have much difficulty in eating the amount of food required for foetal growth, but when there are four or more puppies in the uterus they occupy more and more of the abdomen as pregnancy progresses. The amount of food that can be eaten at one meal is limited to the space the stomach can expand to fill. You can therefore expect your bitch to eat smaller meals but more often, and during the last week she may need to be fed during the night. By the last week of pregnancy it is not unusual for the food intake to be increased to 50–60 per cent over the level before mating.

Offer a balanced diet, feed to appetite, give a calcium supplement over the last three weeks and you will not go far wrong.

Exercise during pregnancy

During the first six weeks of pregnancy exercise can be virtually as before, but as the bitch starts getting heavier she will limit her exercise to her capability. It is obvious that no pregnant bitch should dash madly around chasing balls once she reaches the half-way mark. It will be equally obvious to her, so she will start to take things more slowly. Gentle walks are good for her providing she is ready for them.

Preparing for whelping

Your bitch should have a place set aside for whelping that provides peace and quiet, privacy, warmth and freedom from draughts without being stuffy. This is unlikely to be possible in her usual sleeping area if she lives indoors, especially so in a smallish kitchen.

If she is to whelp somewhere that she does not usually 'live', she must be acclimatized to it before whelping starts. Get the site and the whelping box ready in good time so that she can be introduced to them, given her food there and generally prepared for the big day, or night.

The whelping box

The whelping box is designed to provide the bitch with enough room to lie full length in any direction, which should mean that there will be enough room for the litter as well in the first four or five weeks of their life. There is no need to rush off to the pet store to buy a custom-made box with all mod cons. You can easily make one yourself.

Three sides of the box should be as high as the bitch is wide. The fourth side, which will be the front, should be about one-third of that height. This will permit the bitch to move in and out without any problem but keep the puppies in a restricted area until they are able to fend

five minutes fun and now look at me!

for themselves a little. Wood is a perfectly satisfactory material for the construction of whelping boxes but it is *not* advisable to lend (or borrow) wooden ones. They are not easily disinfected and it is always much wiser not to tempt providence.

In the very small breeds an ideal and economical whelping box can be adapted from cardboard cartons. They have the added attraction of being both expendable and hygienic. The important thing is to ensure continuity of supply as cartons do not last very long once a litter of pups starts performing in them. Any box will do providing it is big enough for the dimensions given above. The design for the front can be a circular hole, large enough for the bitch to go through with ease but high enough to keep the puppies inside.

The bedding

The bedding should be expendable and easily changed and replaced. Your bitch would be delighted to use the best mink in the house but will be equally happy with newspaper. If you have not got a store of newspapers then beg or borrow some from your friends. It is unlikely they will want them back, actually, especially when you tell them what you want them for!

Heating

During the summer months the need for heating will be reduced but should not be forgotten or ignored, just in case there is not a heatwave at the time. It is not that the bitch needs to be kept particularly warm during whelping but the puppies will when they slip out of an environment of 101.5 °F (38.6 °C) into the cold world outside. Aim for a temperature of 75–80 °F (24–26.5 °C) in the whelping box area. An infra-red lamp over the box is ideal but do ensure it is not so close that it cooks the bitch. Now – get ready, steady, GO!

Whelping

There are three stages of labour, but it is not always easy to tell when the first stops and the second begins until the arrival of the first pup tells you that the second stage had started earlier than you thought.

Stage one

This is the time when the uterus begins to exert pressure and, as a result, the cervix begins to relax and open up. The bitch becomes restless, starts making a bed and begins to pant. Some bitches may start bed-making a day or so earlier but without the other signs. That is not indicative of the onset of the first stage.

The duration of the first stage is about 8–12 hours but can be shorter or even as long as 72 hours. In the well-adapted pet this stage is not prolonged, but the neurotic pet (probably with a neurotic owner) can be so upset that relaxation of the cervix is inhibited and some sedation is desirable, preferably for the owner but certainly for the dog!

The signs described start off at a low intensity and should gradually become more intense as time goes on. If they do not change in intensity nor in frequency then there is a fair chance the bitch has uterine inertia (where the uterus is not contracting). If the uterus does not contract, the cervix will not open. If the cervix does not open how are the puppies going to come out? If you suspect uterine inertia, or if you do not suspect it but the bitch is not showing growing intensity of signs, consult your vet who can initiate the process by injection.

As the cervix dilates, so the membranes and fluids surrounding the puppy are being pushed backwards through the cervix. Eventually the membranes may burst and a green or greenish-brown discharge be observed at the vulva, but the timing is variable and some puppies may be born with the membranes intact. Once the head of the puppy is engaged in the birth canal, the second stage of labour begins.

That always supposes the puppy is coming head first. About 60–65 per cent of births are head first in the bitch, the other 35–40 per cent being perfectly normal births, but coming backwards, feet first.

Stage two

Once the puppy becomes engaged in the birth canal the real straining efforts associated with the second stage begin and the abdominal muscles are brought in to play. Fluids are voided at intervals and every so often the bitch cleans herself up at the vulva. The agitation of the first stage is superseded by a quieter attitude as the bitch concentrates on contracting. It can be an apparently effortless process in one bitch and cause a certain amount of obvious discomfort in others.

The first pup in a bitch's first litter is usually the one that requires the most effort to be born. Once the birth canal has been stretched by the first pup passing down it, its littermates have a rather easier journey, including those in subsequent pregnancies. After the first puppy is born you should expect the afterbirth (or placenta) to be expelled, although sometimes it is not passed until after the next puppy has emerged. This does not matter, but do keep a count of puppies born and afterbirths expelled. If they do not tally there may be a retained placenta and your vet will have to investigate. Keep an eye on the bitch as she may eat an afterbirth or two without your noticing, or even all of them.

When a puppy is born the foetal membranes may still be intact and cover its head completely. The bitch usually clears them away herself, but if she does not you must do so quickly so that breathing can begin unimpeded.

Occasionally, a puppy may emerge still attached to its afterbirth. Again, the bitch is likely to do something about it, but if not you should separate them for her. The bitch will use her teeth but you will find a sharp pair of sterilized scissors more acceptable. Leave at least 2 in (5 cm) of cord on the pup. There is no need to tie it. If you prefer to tear the cord instead of cutting it, do remember that the tearing should be performed without stretching or pulling between the puppy and your grip on the cord.

The mother usually licks the newborn puppy vigorously, but if she neglects to you must do so instead. There is no need for you to lick it, unless you do not have a clean, warm towel handy to rub it down. Introduce the puppy to the milk supply and mother will usually take care of the rest.

The timing of stage two

The first puppy is usually born within an hour of the bitch starting to experience contractions. If nothing has happened after two hours, contact the vet. The period between one puppy and the next can last anything from a few minutes to three hours of rest followed by another period of straining of around 5 to 30 minutes. As a general rule you should suspect problems if the bitch strains between pups for more than two hours.

Stage three

The third stage of labour is the expulsion of the afterbirth, which has already been touched on during discussion of the second stage. By now you will realize that the birth process is not a simple 1–2–3 sequence of stages, with all the pups coming one after the other in the second stage then all the afterbirths in the third stage. It is almost, but not quite, a 1–2–3 for each pup, with possible permutations like 1–2–1–2–3–3. The more pups there are, the more permutations there can be. However, if you have any suspicion that things are not going well call your vet.

The end of labour

This is the most difficult part for most owners, until they have the experience of a few whelpings behind them. Many owners have thought all was finished, gone to bed, and found more pups in the whelping box than there were when they went to bed. Others have stayed up all night when they could have gained some sleep.

A bitch tends to relax when it is all over and have a gentle snooze. You cannot count on this as a sign that whelping is over but it is a fairly good guide. And now you really can tiptoe away, pour yourself a stiff drink and congratulate yourself on your expertise in canine midwifery.

Post-whelping check

Many breeders are confident in their own judgement and ask the vet to check the bitch only if they think it justified. Others would never miss it out. There is no hard-and-fast rule but it is advisable for the first litter or two, at least – not

the bitch's first few litters, the owner's! It is especially advisable if the whelping and/or pregnancy have been difficult.

Postnatal care

The bitch

The most important things to keep an eye on are the vulva for discharges, the mammary glands for inflammation (mastitis) and the bitch's general well being (appetite, water intake and all the other signs that were discussed earlier).

Any deviation from normal is reason enough to consult the vet, particularly if the litter is a valuable pedigree one. Should you decide to take your bitch's temperature after whelping, be warned that it is usually up to 102–103 °F (38.8–39.4 °C) for 48–72 hours afterwards. Do not attach too much importance to a temperature in that range unless the dog is looking under the weather.

The food intake should be kept up during the lactation. The more milk the puppies take the more the bitch will produce, but she can only do so from the raw materials available. If she is not given enough food to produce the milk she will produce it at her own expense – and lose weight.

A lactating bitch will probably need twice her normal daily ration in the first week after whelping, rising to three times the amount when the pups are a month old. This should be a balanced diet with added calcium and phosphorus to meet the pups' additional demands for those minerals, for teeth and bone formation.

This extra food means at least three meals a day and probably more, even at night. By the time the puppies are three or four weeks old they can be introduced to solid food and will gradually become less dependent on their mother's milk. Her need for food will then decrease.

Mention should be made of one problem that may arise at any time in the first three weeks after whelping. This is eclampsia, caused by a low blood calcium level (although there is really no calcium deficiency, as such). If the bitch is restless, showing anxiety or is nervous and over-excitable, suspect eclampsia. Some dogs may also pant, whine, have muscle tremors and be irritable. This is a serious condition and treatment must not be delayed. The bitch can go into a coma within only 12 hours of the symptoms appearing.

The puppies

The puppies need to get their mother's milk within the first 24 hours to obtain passive immunity from her against those diseases for which she has antibodies. That is the first thing you should make sure of. And if curiosity has not got the better of you already, you can check the sexes now.

If the pups are born with dew claws which you wish to have removed, this is best done when they are two or three days old. Their tails should be docked at the same time, if this is necessary. Both can be done quickly and simply by the vet, although some more experienced breeders do it themselves. This is *not* advisable unless you know exactly what you are doing and, of course, remember to throw the right bit away.

The puppies' eyes open at ten days of age as a general rule. Gradually they move a little further afield and their rate of growth increases rapidly. By the time they are three weeks old you can start to wean them.

Weaning

Weaning is initiated by offering cow's milk and minced meat (beef) in small quantities daily. Alternatively, you can use reputable brands of canned dog foods (even better, puppy foods), perhaps softened with a little water. Commercial foods do at least ensure that the vitamin and mineral balance of the diet is correct.

To begin with you may have to tempt the pups by placing a little food on their tongues. As they begin to take to it, you can serve the food on a flat dish placed conveniently near by.

The puppies' demands on their mother's milk will gradually decrease as they take more solid food. Indeed, the bitch will start to discourage them from suckling and will leave the litter for longer and longer periods. The puppies will be quite independent by about six weeks of age, at which time their first set of teeth will start to come through.

Selling the puppies

Either all your friends are clamouring at the door for one of your puppies or you cannot give them away if you try. Now you know what your friends think of your bitch!

A litter is best split up at about eight weeks of age. Any younger and a pup will not have had time to adjust to its littermates and the conventions of canine society. As a result it may grow up unable to get along with other dogs. Any older, on the other hand, and it may have difficulty in getting along with other people. Before it arrives in a new home a pup should be used to people and a little more than just one room, a whelping box and a few food bowls.

The thoughtful owner will have lined up new homes well in advance and you should aim to do the same. You should also ensure that a pup's new owners are competent to look after it and know what they are letting themselves in for. And if you are *really* responsible you will ensure that the puppies have their first vaccination at least 48 hours before they leave you.

9. The canine cult

The majority of dogs are bought as pets and kept as pets in the home. Others are bought to satisfy a whim of having the best, a status symbol or something to show off, even just to show!

Showing

There is nothing wrong with showing providing it is in the right spirit. Indeed, an increasing number of dogs are being shown by some of the more enterprising owners, especially if they own one of the more enterprising dogs. A show can be a fascinating experience that, once sampled, will have you hooked. Others may find the massed ranks of competitors, canine and human, a nightmare.

Most countries have shows run under the control of the national governing body. In the United Kingdom this is the Kennel Club. It is usual for all shows that the only dogs exhibited are registered in the name of the exhibitor by the governing body, so if you are ever likely to want to show your dog make sure it is registered in your name.

Before you decide, take the trouble to go to a few shows. In Britain there are the Limited Shows which are confined to members of the club or society that has organized them, the Open Shows which are not so restricted and the Championship Shows which are the most important and lead ultimately to the world-famous Crufts Show. Most countries have a very similar type of show circuit.

What to look for

If you have never been to a show it may all seem a little strange at first. The best way is to go with an exhibitor who

already knows the ropes, but if that is not possible you must steel yourself to plunge into the fray and ask as many questions as you can.

The exhibitors arrive with their dogs looking as near their best as the journey permitted. They were certainly in pristine condition the night before. When the exhibitors have settled in they will give their dogs one final treatment, secure the water supply, eye up the competition and wait for the big moment. As soon as the right class is called they will gather their charge and head straight for the ring – you must not keep the judges waiting!

You will already have found a convenient vantage-point. Now watch how the dogs are handled in the ring: the key is to show the dog off at its best without letting it lose interest in the proceedings. Watch what the judges do and ask the exhibitors what they think they are trying to do – although tactfully, of course, if a dog has disgraced itself.

The judges

It may not be apparent at first, but judges are usually experienced exhibitors who have earned the respect of the bodies running the shows and even the other exhibitors. Not that everyone will agree with the judge. All judges are assessing the entries against the breed standards. Those standards are sometimes loose enough to allow a certain amount of latitude in interpretation, not to mention personal opinion. This means that if you disagree with a judge you are unlikely to be able to quote chapter and verse to prove him or her wrong.

Training for shows

You have done your homework by now and spied out the land. You know what is expected of you, but does your dog know what is expected of it? Are you confident that it will be a credit to you?

A few enquiries should succeed in finding suitable dog-training schools and classes in your area. Some, but not all, give ringcraft classes. These are particularly valuable to the novice exhibitor *and* the novice exhibit. Here you can get all the advice you need on how to train your dog to stand for the judges and show itself off to best advantage – and how to show yourself off too.

Preparing for shows

Shows demand a great deal of work: early morning travel and late evening travelling home, either elated with the euphoria that follows a win or sad that this time you had not been placed.

Start by checking over the dog well beforehand to sort out the odd problem with claw-clipping, ear-cleaning and so on (and do not forget to check the teeth early enough to get them scaled if necessary). Then give it a thorough shampoo and brush the day before the show, but do take care not to give it a chill while you are doing so. After that there is little more to do than get everything ready for the journey, keep your fingers crossed and await the happy day.

You will need to take your grooming brushes and combs, food and two bowls (one for water). Do not forget to take food and water (or something stronger) for yourself; sustenance at the show may be hard to come by, or hard to eat. Finally, pack the documents that you will require and your show collar and lead.

On arrival, make sure that you know when and where you are likely to be in the ring and keep calm and cool. If you are nervous or excited, so will your dog be. When your turn does come, remember that the judges are only human and may – although, of course, it will seem very unfair – prefer a different dog from your own. Swallow your pride and resolve to come again – next time you may find another judge who prefers yours.

any case, such drawbacks are scarcely the hound's fault. It was bred originally for field work and once it gets its nose on a scent it has neither eyes to see nor ears to hear. Look on the bright side – at least you will be able to keep up with it.

Best of breeds

There are so many different breeds in the world that it is impossible to cover them all in any book. Those that follow include some of the most popular and/or easy to keep for the novice owner, although like any selection it will probably offend some and disappoint others.

Basset Hound

Like the camel, the Basset Hound (see page 41) is reputed to have been designed by committee. Despite its extraordinary shape, however, it is a lovable character of almost saintly disposition, particularly good with children and affectionate to its master. If this sounds a little too good to be true then it has to be said that Bassets tend to be smelly (they have an oily skin) and hard to train. But persistence will usually win through and, in

Boxer

A popular breed that is good tempered, has a sense of humour (it has to with a face like that) and mixes well with children. However, the popularity of Boxers (see page 42) has led to a degree of mass production and some lines are both unreliable and rather ugly. Be careful in your selection and avoid white specimens altogether – they are deaf. This is a good breed for a family from which you can expect affection and stamina. You can also expect an almighty scrap if it ever gets in a fight – Boxers don't give up.

Dachshund

These come in ordinary and miniature sizes, either long-, smooth- or wire-haired. Dachshunds are playful and responsive dogs, ideal for flats or where there is not a lot of space. They have no objection to being carried everywhere, and frequently are – Dachshunds are typical lapdogs. But do not thereby assume that they need no exercise; they do. With their short legs, overweight Dachshunds resemble nothing so much as a self-propelled sausage – and the propellant does not take them very far.

German Shepherd Dog

Formerly called the Alsatian, the German Shepherd has a reputation for being vicious and dangerous. In general, individuals are only so if they have been trained as guard dogs or brought up by a weak owner and become the pack leader. Many are kind and gentle, but beware of those that are nervous of strangers – you will never be able to trust them. German Shepherds come in short- and long-coated varieties in black and tan, black and gold, sable, cream or white, pure black and a few other colours as well. A properly trained German Shepherd can be as loyal, intelligent and hard-working a dog as any owner could want, providing there is plenty of room to keep it and you buy from breeding stock screened for hip dysplasia.

Irish Setter

Some Irish Setters can be rather unpredictable, dashing madly around in circles and leaping about as if they had a bee on their bottom. Fortunately most are more even tempered and well behaved, and there is no doubt that this can be one of the most elegant and rewarding of breeds. However, Irish Setters do need plenty of exercise daily and care lavished on their beautiful mahogany or chestnut-red coat. If properly kept – and towns do not really suit its natural exuberance – you will find the Irish Setter an engaging companion.

Labrador Retriever

Labradors come in black, gold and chocolate and are to be distinguished from the Golden Retriever, see page 43, a different breed. They can be a little exuberant but are usually very good with children and make ideal family pets as long as you keep the ornaments high enough; they have tails like scythes. Labradors have been bred as gundogs for many years and their working ancestry is reflected in their need for plenty of fresh air and exercise, something to bear in mind if you live in a town. On balance the temperament of the Labrador is good, especially the working lines, and its loyalty and intelligence are first rate. There have been some reports that Labradors figure high on the list of delinquent dogs, but then as one of the most popular breeds they no doubt attract a high proportion of delinquent owners.

Old English Sheepdog

Old English Sheepdogs require a great deal of work to keep them groomed (daily), clean and sweet smelling. There is a popular myth that if the hair around the eyes is cut away they will go blind, but since they can hardly see with the hair occluding their vision it is not surprising that some are inclined to bite when touched unexpectedly. This can happen with any dog but more so with the Old English Sheepdog as it can *never* tell when it is going to be touched! The breed became popular very quickly, with the result that some lines are from poor stock. Choose carefully if you decide to acquire one and remember that this is a large dog that needs plenty of exercise and a firm hand in obedience-training.

Poodles

Poodles come in three sizes: Standard (the largest – see page 42), Miniature (the middle size) and Toy. Despite their reputation for effeteness and sometimes bizarre appearance when clipped, poodles of all kinds are extremely intelligent and have long been one of the most popular breeds. They are good with children, adapt easily to most households and are not particularly demanding in their needs. Being so small, Toy Poodles can lead to difficulties in their uncanny resemblance to fluffy, barrel-shaped cushions. Watch where you sit in any house with one of these.

Spaniels

The blanket term for a variety of breeds. The smallest is the King Charles Spaniel, which comes in a variety of colours. Its appealing, little-child-lost appearance often leads it to be spoiled and outrageously pampered – but you won't find the dog complaining! Among its cousins are the larger Cocker Spaniel which needs proper exercise, and the English Springer Spaniel. The latter is a really splendid dog, good with the family and eager to please, and particularly eager for very long walks.

Terriers

If you find the variety of spaniels confusing, don't even try with terriers. There are more of them than of any other kind of dog. The most popular by far is the Yorkshire terrier; racy show-biz examples are known for their ribbons and diamond-studded collars. 'Yorkies' are, in fact, almost the ideal toy dog, undemanding and needing little exercise. Do not rush to the breeder at once, however. Like all terriers they can be extremely assertive and without a firm hand you will find that that appealing bundle of fluff will grow into a diminutive and snappy canine Mussolini. Other popular breeds are the Cairn, the West Highland White, the Bull Terrier (this one has jaws like a steel trap) and the Jack Russell. The last has not yet been officially accepted as a breed in Britain, but can be of such an assertive and sometimes truculent character that it probably couldn't care less.

Index

Page numbers in italics indicate illustrations.

Picture credits

The publishers are grateful to the following for granting permission to reproduce copyright material: Page 41: Spectrum Colour Library. Pages 42, 43, 44, 93, 94 (below), 95 and 96: ZEFA Picture Library. Page 94 (above): Howard Loxton.